Napkin Theology

Napkin Theology

Small Drawings about Big Ideas

Tyler Hansen

AND

Emily Lund

Illustrated by Jodie Londono

CASCADE *Books* • Eugene, Oregon

NAPKIN THEOLOGY
Small Drawings about Big Ideas

Cascade Books
An Imprint of Wipf and Stock Publishers
199 W. 8th Ave., Suite 3
Eugene, OR 97401

www.wipfandstock.com

PAPERBACK ISBN: 978-1-6667-4785-0
HARDCOVER ISBN: 978-1-6667-4786-7
EBOOK ISBN: 978-1-6667-4787-4

Cataloguing-in-Publication data:

Names: Hansen, Tyler [author]. | Lund, Emily [author]. | Londono, Jodie [illustrator]

Title: Napkin theology : small drawings about big ideas / by Tyler Hansen and Emily Lund, illustrated by Jodie Londono.

Description: Eugene, OR: Cascade Books, 2023 | Includes bibliographical references.

Identifiers: ISBN 978-1-6667-4785-0 (paperback) | ISBN 978-1-6667-4786-7 (hardcover) | ISBN 978-1-6667-4787-4 (ebook)

Subjects: LCSH: Theology, Doctrinal—Popular works. | Theology. | Theology, Doctrinal.

Classification: BT65 H36 2023 (print) | BT65 (ebook)

03/15/23

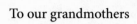

To our grandmothers

Contents

Acknowledgments

Tyler

This book is the product of the many people who have loved me and taught me. My friend Megan Westra told me that writing a book is a way to let others in on the conversations you (the author) have had with many others through the years. This list is by no means exhaustive, but I want to specifically thank a few folks.

Many thanks to my professors at Wheaton College and Northern Seminary. Dr. Jerry Root, thank you for teaching me how much God loves me, and for using napkins and drawings to communicate the richness of the Christian tradition. I'm grateful to you, and I love you. Dr. Beth Felker Jones, thank you for teaching my first theology course in my sophomore year, and for teaching me how to think theologically. Dr. Cherith Fee Nordling, thank you for helping me put all the pieces together theologically, to see myself as an image-bearer. Your fingerprints are all over the human anthropology chapter. You helped me live theologically, and taught me how to write as a worshiper of the triune God.

Thank you to my students at Willow Creek Community Church Wheaton. Working as your youth pastor, praying for you, and encouraging you to follow in the ways of Jesus was one of the great privileges of my life. I have you in my heart.

I want to thank my friends Jordan, Christian, Bennett, Tommy, and Ben. I take great joy in each of you. I am rich because of my friends. Your phone calls and texts and prayers mean more than I can fully express. I'll see you on Memorial Day. Also, thank you to Giannis Antetokounmpo for making basketball relevant in Wisconsin again.

Many thanks to my family. I am who I am because you have loved me. Mom and Dad, Jana and Nate—thank you for modeling what it means to be a Christian in the world. I am a Christian because of your compelling example. Henry and Raymond, I pray you two grow up to be as much friends as you are brothers, and that you would not know a day apart from God's love. Thank you to my aunts and uncles—Andy, Holly, and Jenn. You have always had my back, and know just the right ways to include and encourage me.

And finally, thank you, Emily. You are pure grace to me. You are even better than my dreams. I love you, and I love our little life together. Let's keep having a lot of fun.

Emily

When I first made plans to go to seminary, my hope was to go learn the jargon and "shorthand" of theological studies so I could then leave the world of academia and work to create rich, readable resources for people of faith. It is such an honor and joy to see those hopes becoming reality.

At Duke Divinity School, I was privileged to sit in the classrooms of some of the sharpest minds in the fields of theology and biblical studies, whose insights and instruction all appear in this book. A special thank-you goes to Edgardo Colón-Emeric, whose Christian Theology class provided so many of the key sources and frameworks for my own thinking and for this project, and to Jeremy Begbie, for all of the wisdom and guidance as I worked on my thesis. Thanks are also due to Warren Smith, Ross Wagner, Ellen Davis, Laura Lieber, Susan Eastman, and Janet Soskice. I am so grateful for your teaching.

Thank you, Aleta, for reading the drafts of some of these chapters and providing the perfect pieces of encouragement and advice.

Thank you, Jodie, for agreeing to illustrate this book and responding so well to a whirlwind of emails and questions (and thank you, Curtis, for the introduction!).

Thank you to all our wonderful church folks, who are showing us the meaning and joy of community more and more each week.

Mom and Dad, thank you for the lifelong encouragement in the ways of reading and writing and learning. Thank you, Dad, for typing up the books I dictated to you before I could write. Thank you, Mom, for being my first-ever copy editor and proofreader.

Thank you, Anna, for being the best kind of sister I could want: a friend.

And Ty: we did it! Thank you for letting me go after this idea with you and trusting me with it. Thank you for giving me hope. Thank you for being my best friend, my best "yes." I love you.

Why theology?

Introduction

R ecently, I (Emily) was telling a friend what I'd been learning in my Bible and theology classes when she interrupted me, looking rather embarrassed. "Sorry," she said, "but I have a dumb question. What exactly is the difference between studying the Bible and studying theology? Aren't they kind of the same thing?"

Her question wasn't dumb—far from it. It took me a *very* long time to figure out what theology actually was. Unless you go to seminary or preach every week, it's not really a word you hear that often.

But here's the thing: even if you can't describe what theology is, even if you've never heard the word before, you have still practiced theology at some point in your life.

So what is theology, anyway?

The word "theology" might conjure up images of bearded men with glasses who probably died a few centuries ago, poring over biblical commentaries and thinking Deep Thoughts. It might sound reminiscent of "biology" or "anthropology" or any number of "ologies" you've been forced to study.

In other words: it might not sound like something interesting, or relevant, or especially useful.

Yes, you'll find a lot of bearded men (some of them with glasses) when you study theology. And yes, it is an "ology"—a field of study. When you start breaking the word apart even further, though, it doesn't sound too bad.

Our word "theology" comes from two other words, ancient Greek words: *theos* and *logos*. *Theos* means "God." *Logos* means "word." It's the same word used in the famous first verse of John's Gospel: "In the beginning was the Word, and the Word was with God, and the Word was God."

Think of theology as a simple equation: God + word.

At its most basic level, theology is words and God, God and words. It's words *to* God, words *from* God. It can also be words *about* God, which is often what people think theology is all about (remember the bearded men reading and thinking Deep Thoughts?). Really, however, theology is "God talk"—whether it's God talking to us, us talking to God, or us talking about God and things related to God.

Of course, in practice, it's a little more complicated. There are plenty of fancy terms and complicated lines of thinking to describe everything from creation to the last judgment (and everything in between). Theologians have developed a kind of shorthand to reference all the concepts and ideas they discuss. And unfortunately, that shorthand means a lot of people intrigued by God and the church think that theology is way too "academic," way too "heady" for them to ever really understand it (or even be interested in it).

But think back to that most basic definition. Theology is "God talk"—which means that if you've ever talked about God or talked to God, then you've done your own kind of theological work, no matter how small it may seem. Even if you've never set foot in a seminary class, even if you've never read Augustine or Aquinas or Barth—and even if you've never heard of them—you've taken part in the world of theology.

If we're already doing it, then why study it?

Theology can actually make your life better.

Really—hang with us here. The point of knowing things about theology is not to memorize terms and names so you can impress your friends or achieve a certain level of nerddom. The point of knowing anything about theology is so you can translate that *knowing* into *doing*, and more specifically *following*: following Jesus.

There's a theologian named Beth Felker Jones who talks about how theology is primarily about becoming Jesus' disciples. She writes that "we learn to speak and think well about God so that we can be more faithful followers of Jesus."[1] Theology, in its most basic sense, is "words + God." Theology in its *fullest* sense is "words + God for the church, for the Christian." If theology is not done with the intention of guiding believers into the ways of Jesus, it's incomplete. It's missing a vital element: faith.

People of faith need theology—good, sound, robust theology. You've probably heard the saying that goes "bad company corrupts good character." Bad theology corrupts, well, everything. Throughout history, people have twisted their God-talk to justify all kinds of terrible things, from slavery to murder to domestic abuse. Right God-talk is needed to fight against that. It's also needed to encourage fellow believers, to remind each other of what is true about our God.

We'll discuss this more in the conversation about the theological term "revelation," because many of the words we receive from God were first designed for a different audience than people today, in the twenty-first century. In theology, we often overhear other conversations, and we must be sensitive to that. For example, in the New Testament, we can read the apostle Paul's letters to his protégé Timothy. And, well, we're not Timothy—but we are the grateful recipients of that letter, which Christians before us deemed necessary to preserve. If we become arrogant and think that every word written throughout history is written directly to us, then it increases the chances that our God-talk won't be accurate.

Studying theology gives us the humbling, exciting opportunity to study God and the things of God. It's intensely personal—because when we study those things, we learn more and more about our own story. We learn about where we came from, where we're going. We learn about the stains of sin that mar our lives. We learn about the God who saves and sustains us.

And all these ideas and concepts are interconnected—webs of thought, woven together.

You can't study where we came from in the doctrines of creation without also thinking about the reality of sin: or, in technical terms, diving into some *hamartiology*. Thinking about doctrines of salvation means you'll probably also think about *eschatology*: the field of study that deals with the last things, with where this whole universe is eventually going. It's all part of this messy, wonderful feast of ideas that we call theology.

The book you hold in your hands is designed to make your approach to the table a little less daunting.

---

1. Jones, *Practicing Christian Doctrine*, 13.

Hence the napkins.

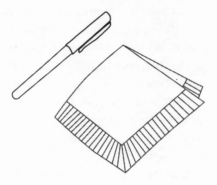

When Tyler was a youth pastor and students would ask him questions about God and salvation and sin, he'd sometimes pull out a pen and a napkin. (He first learned this from his pastors and professors!) He'd draw a picture as he talked about their question, scribbling arrows and stick figures to help both him and the student understand the words a bit better.

Now Ty is a big believer in napkin theology—because theology is far from being the Ivy-League, ivory-tower thing so many people think it is. Theology involves so much of what we think about, sometimes on a daily basis: "What's God up to? Why are we here? What's this world all about?"

Napkin theology isn't supposed to replace the big books and long lectures that address these same questions. But it *is* supposed to show that the most profound truths are much more accessible than we think they are.

Now go grab a pen and a napkin from the stack in your kitchen, or one of those Starbucks napkins that's sitting in your car console. It's time to start drawing.

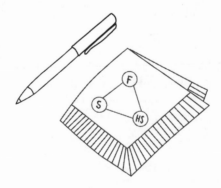

1

So who are we talking about?

The triune God

A ny book about the things of God should probably begin by answering the question "Who is God?" Within the Christian tradition, the answer is that God is the One who loves as Father, Son, and Holy Spirit. This is the doctrine of the Trinity: God is three in one. Really, whenever we say "God," we're using a shortcut word for "Father, Son, and Holy Spirit."

Admittedly, this can get a bit complicated. Christians say that they only have *one* God, but this seems a whole lot like *three* "gods," doesn't it?

Before we get ahead of ourselves in explaining the mystery and beauty of the triune God, maybe a picture will help.

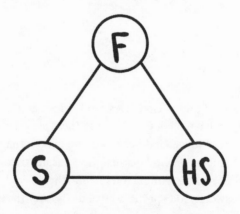

Father, Son, and Spirit are the three *persons* of the Trinity. (Not "objects," not "parts," not "sections": *persons*. It's the way Christians have decided that God-talk about the Trinity should go.) These are not three separate gods. They are so interconnected in love that they are of one single substance.

Before we can say anything else about God, we must first say this: God loves God's own self. The Father loves the Son, and the Son loves the Spirit. The Spirit loves the Father, and the Father loves the Spirit. The Son loves the Father, and—you get the point. We like the way the theologian Thomas Torrance writes about who God is and what the doctrine of the Trinity means: "This is what the doctrine of the Holy Trinity supremely means, that God himself is Love. This is not a static unmoved and unmoving Love, for God's Being is an eternal movement in Love, and consists in the Love with which the Father, the Son and the Holy Spirit ceaselessly love one another."[1]

It makes sense, then, that when we sketch God, we should include a heart, which represents the love at the core of God's life.

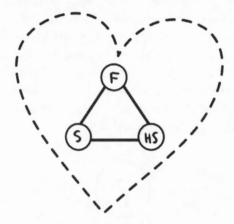

God does a lot of things. God saves, God judges, and God creates—but those are all things that God does for others. These are *external* to God, not *internal*. God cannot judge God because there is no wrongdoing in God; God cannot have mercy on God because God has never committed an offense that requires mercy. Within God's being, there is only love, which is why Christians say that God's primary attribute is love. The theologian Karl Barth writes, "'God is' means 'God loves.' . . . All our further insights about who and what God is must revolve round this mystery—the mystery of His

1. Torrance, *The Christian Doctrine of God*, 162–63.

loving. In a certain sense they can only be repetitions and amplifications of the one statement that 'God loves.'"[2]

When some of the first Christians began to think about who God was, they asked a question: "Before God was creating the world, what was God doing?" The answer they came to, in short, was this: God was enjoying God's self. These Christians began to use a Greek word, *perichoresis*, to describe the love that the Father, Son, and Holy Spirit have had for one another from eternity past, long before the universe was created. This word is difficult to precisely translate into English, but it means something like "delight," "mutual indwelling," or "endless joy." *Perichoresis* is a word we use to try and capture the idea that within the life of the Father, Son, and Holy Spirit, there is complete and unstoppable joy.

That's why we've inserted these arrows between the three persons of the Trinity—they communicate that God's life is not static or stale. God's life is charged with an endless movement of love and joy.

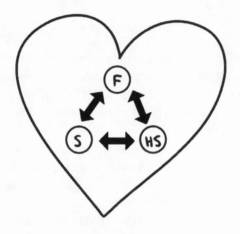

The biblical witness

The actual word "Trinity" doesn't appear in the Bible. But that doesn't mean we can't see glimpses of the triune God when we read Scripture.

My (Tyler's) favorite is the story of Jesus' baptism. Saint Matthew writes, "And when Jesus had been baptized, just as he came up from the water, suddenly the heavens were opened to him and he saw the Spirit

2. Barth, *CD* 2/1:283–84.

of God descending like a dove and alighting on him. And a voice from heaven said, 'This is my Son, the Beloved, with whom I am well pleased'" (Matt 3:16–17).

When Jesus was baptized, God gave us a peek at what kind of love exists in the life of the triune God. All three persons of the Trinity are distinct and separate, yet they share the same substance. They express their unity in love and joy. In love, the Holy Spirit shines on Jesus. The Holy Spirit wants to let others see Jesus in his glory and power; the Spirit is not selfish. Likewise, when the Father speaks, he doesn't brag about himself; the Father praises the Son, declaring his lavish love. The story of the baptism of Jesus shows that his earthly ministry is empowered by the Holy Spirit and guided by the faithful Father. Jesus does nothing independently of the other persons of the Trinity. When Jesus is baptized, God pulls back the curtains and allows us, creatures who are not God, to see a bit of the love and joy that God has for Godself.

A balancing act

The doctrine of the Trinity requires a good deal of balance, which is why we like to think of speaking properly about God as being on a balance beam. If we emphasize the fact that God is "three" too much, we fail to accurately speak about God, but if we talk about God as "one" too much, then we fall to the other side.

Some Christians have emphasized the "oneness" of God at the expense of "threeness." For them, God is one—but God only *acts* as three different persons. This false idea (which is technically called modalism) is sort of like having a God who wears three different masks. Sometimes, this one God wears the mask and takes on the role of the Holy Spirit, and other times, God plays the role of the Father. The problem with this idea, though, is that if God exists in three modes but is essentially one God, then God is not defined by relational love for God's self. If we fall too far on this side of the balance beam, then we aren't speaking of the true God—because God exists as three persons in loving relationship, not as a single, static deity that plays different roles.

On the other hand, sometimes people go too far to the other extreme of speaking of the persons of the Trinity in a way that emphasizes the "threeness" of God. Sometimes, people are content to have the Father be God, but the Son and the Holy Spirit are only "sort of like God." This false idea is called subordinationism. According to this idea, the Son is subordinate to the Father; the Father is the real God. The problem with this idea is that it makes Jesus "less than God."

The idea of the Trinity is a notoriously difficult one to grasp. And really, that's the point. As St. Augustine once (supposedly) said, "God is not what you imagine or what you think you understand. If you understand, you have failed."

This teaches us a very important lesson about theology: far too often, when we try to have God "make sense," we end up with an inaccurate, unfaithful picture of God. There is nothing in the world that is perfectly one and three at the same time. As people who learn about God, it isn't our job to make God fit into the categories we create. Instead, it is our job to faithfully listen to God and others and allow God to rehabilitate our conceptions of God.

But here's the nice thing about a balance beam: if you fall, there's padding on the ground to protect you. Sometimes people lose their balance and fall to one side of expressing one part of God at the expense of another. (This happens to all of us at one point or another. Trust us—we've had a lot of friends and professors correct us on some wrong beliefs before!) If you ever fall off the balance beam of speaking well of God, that doesn't mean you're a failure. It just means you are fortunate to have brothers and sisters to help you see God accurately. Nobody has all the right answers; we need one another to help us see the full, rich, delightful picture of who God is.

Even though there is nothing in the world that is exactly like the triune God, some helpful metaphors can help us make better sense of who God is.

The theologian and musician Jeremy Begbie, for instance, gives us a helpful way to think about the Trinity—even if we can't ever fully understand it.[3] Think of a chord played on a piano, like this one:

---

3. Begbie, "How Music Helps Explain the Trinity."

When you hear this chord played, you can hear the individual notes: the C, the E, the G. But there is also a unity to it, a full and rich sound of oneness. A simple chord, played on the piano, helps us listen in for a moment to what the mystery of the Trinity might sound like. The three persons do not eclipse or shadow each other—they allow the others to ring out all the more glorious.

Toxic theology: how to avoid it

We need others to correct our errors, because sometimes bad theology can have harmful effects in our lives.

For example, some Christians throughout history have slipped off the balance beam of proper "God-talk" and said that the Son, Jesus Christ, is subordinate to the Father. (This conclusion is reached by way of some verses in the Gospel of John when Jesus says that he only does the will of the Father. Jesus, while certainly obedient, is not subordinate or "less-than.") Some who follow this theology also try to apply analogous thinking to human relationships: as Christ submits to the Father, so women submit to men. (This idea draws on a particular—and highly contested—interpretation of 1 Corinthians 11:3.)

Within the Trinity, the Father, Son, and Holy Spirit take great joy in one another; there is only love that seeks the good of others. Recall the story of Jesus' baptism—there is no hierarchy or jockeying for power. For God, there is only mutual love and joy. Properly speaking of God as the One who loves as Father, Son, and Holy Spirit protects us from using bad theology to, among other things, subordinate women to men.

Another example of bad trinitarian theology is the common conception of God as a stoic, white-bearded man up in the sky. First of all, God is not a man (and does not have a beard, no matter what that famous Michelangelo painting might make you believe). And second of all, God is not an isolated, lonely being. If we fall into the trap of thinking that God is "the man upstairs," we can easily succumb to the idea that we must please this God, to live our lives just right so that God doesn't get angry at us. According to Christian belief, this couldn't be further from the truth. God isn't a man, and God isn't a woman—God is, well, *God*. And this God is happy in God's own life—Father, Son, and Holy Spirit exist in endless joy. (Remember the whole *perichoresis* thing?) Because of this, we can drop the notion of God as a white-bearded man we have to try to please so that he won't smite us.

When I (Tyler) was a freshman in college, a professor and mentor of mine first taught me that God is the One who loves as Father, Son, and Spirit. Growing up, I was lucky to have parents and pastors who told me that God loved me, and I believed them. But somewhere in the back of my mind, I feared that God would be extremely disappointed if my prayers lacked passion or if I did something really bad. Over many breakfasts at the same table in the back corner of my college's dining hall, my professor made it quite clear that none of my positive performances or abysmal failures could increase or decrease God's love. He told me he knew this because God doesn't just choose to love—God *is* love.

The doctrine of the Trinity teaches us that we are not responsible for God's happiness or fulfilling God's emotional needs. Instead, as my friend and professor Cherith Nordling likes to say, we are free to be co-lovers of God. God already loves God's self, and the task of human beings isn't to make God happy: it is to join in God's happiness. When we properly speak of God and worship God for who God is—the one who loves as Father, Son, and Holy Spirit—we have a much better chance at avoiding toxic theology and practice.

The truth that God is love in three persons is good news for us all. God's fundamental demeanor is that of goodness, love, and kindness. If you've ever wondered whether you're making God happy or disappointing God, the doctrine of the Trinity reminds us that none of our success can make God happier, and that none of our failures can change who God is. God is love, and we cannot add to or subtract from that.

But the love of the Father, Son, and Holy Spirit isn't just for God. Instead, God chooses to extend this great love to that which is not God. God *creates*.

2

A world made out of love

Creation

W hen we talk about the Trinity, we talk about love: the three persons of Father, Son, and Holy Spirit in an ever-moving, ever-giving dance of love.

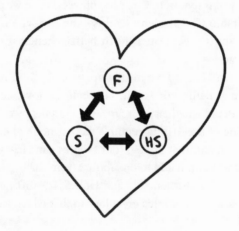

When we talk about creation, we also talk about love: the love amongst the three persons that spilled out into sun and sea and you and me.

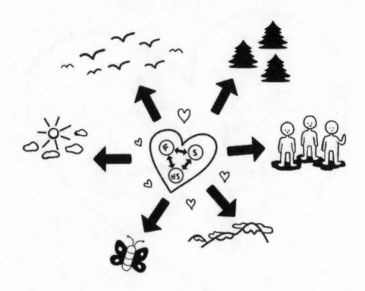

Theology has a couple different terms to talk about these loves and how the Trinity works in relation to itself and in relation to what has been created.

When we think about that dance of love that Father, Son, and Spirit spin and move in, the inner life of these three persons, we are thinking about the *immanent Trinity*. When we say "immanent," we mean "internal," "innate," "inside." This is a pretty mysterious concept, because there's only so much we can know and say about what goes on inside the Godhead apart from what we can see in the world around us.

But we *can* say a few important things. The apostle John put it neatly in his first letter to some early Christians: "Whoever does not love does not know God, for God is love" (1 John 4:8). God does not simply *have* love, or *give* love. Love is not simply an attribute of God; it's God's whole being.

And God chose to allow that love to burst out of God's very own self.

9

"When God began to create the heavens and the earth . . ."

This is where we begin to see the *economic Trinity* at play—the Trinity in its relation to what is not God, in relation to what God has created. God could have chosen to just remain as the immanent Trinity forever, having nothing to do with that which is not God. The love flowing freely between the persons of the Trinity would have been enough for God. Father, Son, and Spirit were not sitting around sulky, moping, in need of praise and adoration.

Creation wasn't necessary.

Our world did not *need* to exist. Everything we see and smell and taste is excessive: an outpouring of God's love. God didn't need to create humans or frogs or planets to satisfy some whim or to appease some lack. God didn't *need* us.

But God *wanted* us.

There's a phrase attributed to St. Augustine: *Amo; volo ut sis*. Translated from Latin, it reads: "I love you; I want you to be." Imagine, for a moment, God whispering this as the heavens and the earth began to take their shape, as Adam was formed from the dust and breathed into life. "I love you; I want you to be."

God needs nothing—but God wants us to be. And in creation, God wanted to share the love that is God's own self and being. In creating, the love within the Trinity flooded over into every nook and cranny of the cosmos, every inch drenched in it.

". . . the earth was complete chaos, and darkness covered the face of the deep . . ."

So God didn't *need* to create, but God *chose* to, freely. That's a statement we need to make when we talk about creation. There's another piece to it, though: that God created *out of nothing*.

When we humans "create," we use paints, bricks, computers, thoughts in our minds: things that already exist. When God created (in the truest sense of that word), God used . . . nothing.

The term theologians use to describe this concept is (you guessed it) a Latin phrase, *creatio ex nihilo*, which translates to "creation out of nothing." This sets God apart from any one of us, and it sets God far beyond the reaches of any technology or tool we might develop. Only God can take nothing—a void of voids—and create.

The scholar Janet Soskice puts it like this: "*Creatio ex nihilo* affirms that God, from no compulsion or necessity, created the world out of nothing—really nothing—no preexistent matter, space, or time."[1] This concept of "really nothing" is essentially impossible for us to fathom. How can we imagine this kind of emptiness? What *creatio ex nihilo* does is force us to confess just how transcendent, just how "other," God is.

But it also shows us another key thing about God.

Many centuries ago, in an English town called Norwich, a woman lived inside a church.

The woman, who became known as Julian of Norwich, lived the life of an "anchoress," voluntarily secluding herself in a cell within the church walls so she could devote herself to prayer and worship.

She spent many years there, sifting through and making sense of some remarkable things that had happened to her. She wrote a book, *Revelations of Divine Love*—the first book written by a woman in the English language—about a series of "showings" she had received from God during a severe

1. Soskice, "Why *Creatio ex nihilo*," 38.

illness. These showings were often dramatic and graphic, showing the suffering Christ in vivid detail, but one of them included a simple image.

> And in this vision he also showed a little thing, the size of a hazel-nut, lying in the palm of my hand, and it was as round as a ball, as it seemed to me. I looked at it and thought, "What can this be?" And the answer came to me in a general way, like this, "It is all that is made." I wondered how it could last, for it seemed to me so small that it might have disintegrated suddenly into nothingness. And I was answered in my understanding, "It lasts, and always will, because God loves it; and in the same way everything has its being through the love of God."[2]

God is transcendent and "other," yes. But God also knows us and sustains us in a profound and personal way. This is not a watchmaker God that some philosophers have spoken of: a God who puts together a watch and then steps back to let it tick away. God is not aloof. We last because God loves us. We couldn't exist without that love—the enveloping love of a God who is both utterly beyond us and beside us.

To emphasize that God sustains us and all of creation, theologians often reference the idea of *creatio continua*, another fancy Latin phrase that means that God constantly upholds all of creation.

God did not simply, at one time, desire to create the world. God always wants the world; he consistently calls what he made "good." God

---

2. Julian of Norwich, *Revelations*, 7.

actively re-creates the world in every single moment. God always wants us, and everything, to be.

What happens when we start to forget some of these ideas about creation?

Much of Christian theology ends up being centered around the person and work of Jesus Christ—which makes sense, considering the name "Christian." The attention we give him is well-deserved, after all. But sometimes the way that focus plays out results in some long-term damage—like when the doctrine of creation starts getting squashed.

A weak theology of creation is bad news for creation. If we focus so much of our energy on ourselves as humans, on what God has done for *us*, and we don't pay much attention to the rest of the universe that God made, we end up staring at a tiny piece of the big picture that is God's love and care for the world.

A Native American theologian named George Tinker knows this all too well. He writes about the ways Christian missionaries preached the gospel to Native Americans, giving it the usual Western-church spin of humanity's fall from grace, their sinful nature, and their need for redemption. For traditionally oppressed and marginalized peoples, however, the emphasis on humanity's sin and their need for a savior doesn't sound like the best news. "Unfortunately," Tinker writes, "by the time the preacher gets to the 'good news' of the gospel, people are so bogged down . . . in [their] internalization of brokenness and lack of self-worth that too often they never quite hear the proclamation of 'good news' in any actualized, existential sense."[3]

Tinker calls for us to start sharing the good news from, well, the *beginning* of it all: that first "in the beginning." He asks for us to "take creation seriously as the starting point for theology rather than treat it merely as an add-on to concerns for justice and peace."[4]

When we begin to neglect the significance of creation—what it says about God and God's love—we can find ourselves getting so wrapped up in our own lost-ness and need that we forget just how loved we have always been, just how valuable everything and everyone around us is. When our theology becomes centered on "just Jesus and me," our sisters and brothers—our whole planet—suffers.

What might it look like to take creation seriously, then—to remember how God holds us tight and close, wanting us to be?

What might it look like to remember that we live in a world that God wants?

God's creation is vast and expansive. God does not choose to be God only for God's own self—God is the One who delights in extending love and life to others. God's good world—created and sustained by God's loving-kindness—is worth knowing and celebrating and protecting.

Luckily for us, God chooses to *reveal* to us more of what we, creation, and God are like. That's what we'll look at in the next chapter.

3. Tinker, "Creation," 42.
4. Tinker, "Creation," 37.

3

Why—and how—does God tell us about God's self?

Revelation

Sometimes, when Christians hear the word "revelation," they think of the last book of the Bible—the one filled with bizarre visions that has spawned the even-more-bizarre interpretations of televangelists.

But "revelation," theologically speaking, is far more than the preferred literature of doomsday preppers.

Revelation is a catch-all word that encapsulates *how* and *why* God tells us about reality.

In those first drawings about who God is back in the Trinity chapter, we learned that God is the One who loves: as Father, Son, and Holy Spirit. In the drawings about creation, we learned that God's love extends to that which is not God (namely: you, us, everyone, everything). Revelation is the way God chooses to communicate this love to us. Before God's self-revelation, we cannot see or know God. We also cannot see or know God's creation, or even the pinnacle of God's creation: humankind.

Without revelation, we find ourselves in a big cardboard box with tape sealing the top.

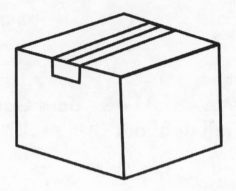

Luckily for us, God loves us so much that God gets rid of the tape. God removes the barriers that impede our knowledge.

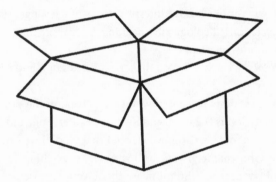

Revelation, therefore, is about far more than simply knowing facts *about* God. It is about actually knowing *God*.

To understand the richness of the revelation of God's own self, we need to ask (and answer) the following questions: *How* does God reveal this knowledge to human beings? And *why* does God do it at all?

First: how?

When God rips off the tape and removes the barriers to our vision—helping us to properly see, know, and love—God does not do so with a single tool. Instead, God uses multiple means to show us reality as it is.

God's revelation comes to us in four primary ways:

1. Jesus Christ
2. The Bible
3. Sacred tradition
4. General revelation

All four ways have some pros and cons (which we'll get to soon!), but first, we need to explain what all four have in common. Each method of revelation is an act of God's *accommodation* to us.

"Accommodation" basically means this: since we human beings are *very* different from God, God's revelation comes to us in ways that are appropriate and understandable to our human minds. The sixteenth-century French theologian John Calvin writes,

> God, in so speaking, lisps with us as nurses are wont to do with little children[.] Such modes of expression, therefore, do not so much express what kind of a being God is, as accommodate the knowledge of him to our feebleness.[1]

Calvin reminds us that all of God's revelation to us is like a nurse "lisping" or "babbling" with a baby. A baby can't really understand the language of adults, so loving parents coo, giggle, smile, and snuggle the baby to communicate that the child is safe, cared for, and loved.

Likewise, human beings cannot fully grasp the mysteries of God, but God speaks to us in ways that are appropriate for our finite minds. Since human beings primarily gain knowledge through experience, history, and reason, God's revelation accommodates itself to us by coming to us in precisely these ways.

Now that we recognize how God accommodates God's self through revelation, let's take a closer look at the four ways that revelation comes to us.

1. Calvin, *Institutes*, 66.

Jesus Christ

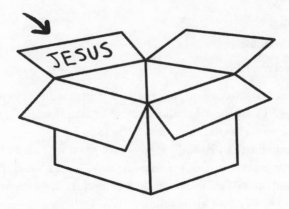

The most obvious means of God's revelation is through Jesus, the Second Person of the Trinity. If "revelation" means the way God communicates to us, then who better to tell us about God than *God himself, in the person of Jesus!*

Take the Gospel of John. John is littered with examples of how Jesus shows us what God is like. John 1:18 reads, "No one has ever seen God. It is the only Son, himself God, who is close to the Father's heart, who has made him known." Basically, if you want to know what God is like, pay attention to Jesus. You get to know a friend by listening to them and spending time together—and you get to know God by getting to know Jesus, by listening to him and spending time with him.

If this seems like an outlandish claim, then you aren't alone. Even Jesus' disciples had trouble accepting the fact that Jesus is, as St. Paul writes, "the image of the invisible God" (Col 1:15). At his final meal with his disciples (after spending three years together!), Jesus says to them, "If you know me, you will know my Father also. From now on you do know him and have seen him." But Philip, one of the twelve disciples, clearly misses the point. "Lord, show us the Father, and we will be satisfied," he says. Jesus answers: "Have I been with you all this time, Philip, and you still do not know me? Whoever has seen me has seen the Father. How can you say, 'Show us the Father'? Do you not believe that I am in the Father and the Father is in me?" (John 14:7–10a). Jesus is the fullness of the triune God—in a human person.

Human beings come to know things by way of our senses: our ability to see, touch, smell, hear, and taste. In Jesus, God's revelation reaches our physical senses. In Jesus, people saw God eat with outcasts and heal the sick. They heard him preach like no one else they'd heard before, and they smelled his sweat when he returned from the wilderness. We can get a taste of Jesus when we take Communion, eating his body and drinking his blood. In hope, we look forward to the day when Jesus will embrace us with his arms, wipe the tears from our cheeks and the sweat from our brows, and let us rest our weary heads on his shoulder.

Finally, God's revelation in Jesus reveals a great kindness of God: we do not need to pursue knowledge of God with fist-clenched, tight-knuckled, all-out effort. God sees the box we're in that limits our view of things as they really are. Jesus stoops down to help open the box and allow us to see.

Karl Barth, the twentieth-century Swiss theologian, writes about this very idea:

> We do not need to engage in a free-ranging investigation to seek out and construct who and what God truly is, and who and what man truly is, but only to read the truth about both where it resides, namely, in the fullness of their togetherness, their covenant which proclaims itself in Jesus Christ.[2]

To know God, we don't need to try to smash the walls that inhibit our sight. Knowing God is as simple as praying to Jesus and reading about him, growing ever closer to him through another means of God's revelation: the Bible.

---

2. Barth, "The Humanity of God," 47.

Scripture

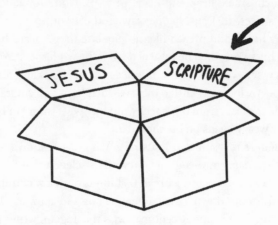

The Bible is the sacred literature of Christianity—and it is another way God reveals God's self to us.

The Christian Scriptures are composed of the Hebrew Bible (or what Christians sometimes call "the Old Testament") and the New Testament. It is important to know that even though the Bible is the holy book for Christians, it actually is more like a library than a book. The Bible is made up of sixty-six individual books written in different time periods, languages, and genres. It is a remarkable piece of literature that describes God's past, present, and future actions. The acts of God recorded in the Bible show us what God is like. When we read the Bible, we are reading what God wants us to know about God's self.

God's revelation in the Bible is *authoritative.* This means that Christians should not (and do not need to) make up their own ideas of what God is like or how we should live. What the biblical writers say of God is enough. With humility, we can read the Bible, accept God's revelation, and let God's words about God shape our imaginations when we think of God. And when the teachings of Scripture reveal to us what it means to live a good life, we can trust and follow that God is revealing the best ways of living for us.

Let's hear from John Calvin once again. He uses a helpful metaphor for us to understand God's revelation through Scripture. He writes:

> For as an eye, either dimmed by age or weakened by any other
> cause, sees nothing distinctly without the aid of glasses, so . . . if

Scripture does not direct us in our inquiries after God, we immediately turn vain in our imaginations.[3]

The world is a bit too wonderful, a bit too complex, for our feeble eyes. Scripture, though, is quite clear. Calvin's metaphor reminds us that our eyes, unaided by God, cannot properly perceive reality. Scripture is what gives us clear vision. What was once obscure comes into clear focus.

Much of Scripture is remarkably and irrefutably clear. But other parts of Scripture tend to get complicated—much more complicated. In order to make sense of the vast record of Scripture, there is a third way we can receive God's revelation: sacred tradition.

Tradition

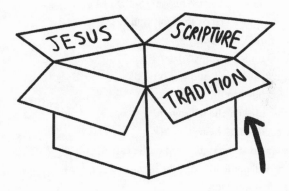

Sacred tradition is the accumulated thought and wisdom of the brothers and sisters who have gone before us in the faith. This tradition exists because the other means of God's revelation (like the Bible) can sometimes get, well, confusing.

But right away, let's be clear: the random opinions of particular Christians do not count as "sacred tradition." What distinguishes sacred tradition from someone's Twitter insight is that sacred tradition has to be agreed upon by *a lot* of people over a *long period* of time.

For example, think about what we talked about back in chapter 1: the doctrine of the Trinity. Even though Jesus himself talks often of "his Father" and promises the gift of "the Holy Spirit," Jesus doesn't *explicitly* outline the doctrine of the Trinity. The Bible does not have any passage that explicitly

3. Calvin, *Institutes*, 91.

says, "God eternally exists as three co-equal persons: Father, Son, and Holy Spirit." This doesn't mean that what God revealed in Scripture is insufficient. It's just that some things God revealed require us to use the logical reasoning that God gave us in our wonderful brains to make sense of God's revelation. It took faithful Christians nearly three hundred years to formulate exactly what Christians mean when we say that God is triune.

One of the most essential writings of the church's tradition is called the Apostle's Creed. Many churches recite these words every single week to remind them of the truth of the Christian faith. This creed—a document written by early church bishops—has now become a source of God's revelation through the sacred tradition of the church. It goes like this:

> I believe in God, the Father almighty,
> creator of heaven and earth.
> I believe in Jesus Christ, his only Son, our Lord,
> who was conceived by the Holy Spirit,
> born of the Virgin Mary,
> suffered under Pontius Pilate,
> was crucified, died, and was buried;
> he descended to the dead.
> On the third day he rose again;
> he ascended into heaven,
> he is seated at the right hand of the Father,
> and he will come to judge the living and the dead.
> I believe in the Holy Spirit,
> the holy catholic Church,
> the communion of saints,
> the forgiveness of sins,
> the resurrection of the body,
> and the life everlasting.
> Amen.[4]

The church agrees that these words are a true, accurate representation of the faith. This sort of revelation from God comes to us through the wise and discerning thoughts of those who have come before us.

Last but not least, let's turn to the fourth means of God's revelation: general revelation.

4. Church of England, "Creed."

General revelation

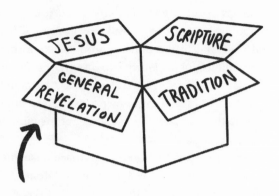

God's revelation also comes to us in ways that, at first glance, don't seem too "spiritual." These ways are often called "general revelation." God's revelation is not confined to Jesus, the Bible, or what theologians agree upon as sacred tradition. God is willing to disclose glimmers of God's self in trees and rivers, in the movie theater and the dining hall, if only we have "a little willingness to see" (as the writer Marilynne Robinson says).[5]

John Calvin (here he is again!) observed, "[God] daily discloses himself in the whole workmanship of the universe" so human beings "cannot open their eyes without being compelled to see him."[6] General revelation corresponds quite logically with creation. Creation is the love of God spilling over into that which is not God, so it makes sense that with love, God chooses to make even the things we typically wouldn't find to be divine or spiritual to contain images, metaphors, or symbols that teach us something of what God is like. Even the biblical writer who penned the nineteenth psalm noticed this medium of God's revelation: "the heavens are telling the glory of God, and the firmament proclaims his handiwork" (Ps 19:1).

General revelation reminds us that God has a penchant for appearing in unexpected places. Oddly enough, God revealed a metaphor for divine love to me (Tyler) when I watched the movie *Lion*.

The protagonist of the movie is a man named Saroo. He was born in India, and through some tragic circumstances, he gets lost, cannot find

5. Robinson, *Gilead*, 289.
6. Johnson, "Metaphysics," 73.

his family, and, in destitution, enters an orphanage to survive. A family from New Zealand adopts him.

As Saroo comes of age, a gnawing sense of curiosity consumes him to learn more about his life in India—all that transpired before he was adopted. Toward the end of the movie, Saroo speaks with his adopted mother about the anguish of his journey to discover his origins, his tragedy, his identity. Saroo appears at a loss. He looks at his adoptive mother and says, "Sorry you couldn't have your own kids." After a dramatic pause, she reveals to Saroo that she could've had kids. Saroo's mother *chooses* to have and to love her son.

This is a moving metaphor for God's love. You and I are not accidents. God *chose* us; God *wants* us. I first saw this movie on a trans-Atlantic flight. I cried gross, snotty tears because of this mother's love that revealed to me the extravagant, unnecessary love of God.

A movie is just one example of general revelation. My (Tyler's) mom sees the depth of God's love in lakes in northern Wisconsin, and my friend Ben senses the order and intentionality of God when he walks through big cities. These are just a couple examples of the normal, ordinary things all around us that speak to the kindness of God.

General revelation requires wisdom, however. We should be careful to not imagine things about God that aren't consistent with what Jesus tells us about God, or that differ from what we find in the Bible or in sacred tradition. If a metaphor or image we think we found about God contradicts something that Jesus did or said, then maybe that was just our imagination. We human beings are not perfect knowers. We require grace, unmerited kindness, in order to have knowledge of God.

Through this process of knowing more and more of God, God removes the barriers to our knowledge, knocking apart the box that keeps us in the dark. Through God's revelation, we human beings move from a self-enclosed box of ourselves into seeing a world that, as the poet Gerard Manley Hopkins put it, "is charged with the grandeur of God."[7]

A word of caution

Revelation is a gift. But like all gifts, it can be spoiled.

---

7. Hopkins, "God's Grandeur."

There is a danger in thinking that by paying attention to Jesus, the Bible, tradition, and general revelation, we can have a monopoly on the truth. When individuals believe they *possess* the truth, ugly arrogance comes next.

A proper understanding of the theology of revelation teaches us that we human beings do not *possess* truth in ourselves. Rather, we *receive* truth from God and *pursue* truth alongside our brothers and sisters. So we should speak about God with the utmost humility, acknowledging that our knowledge of God is incomplete. Only God knows God perfectly. When it comes to speaking faithfully about God, we can have a *sure* word, but never a *final* word. The doctrine of revelation can quickly become toxic if people do not speak of God with gentleness, humility, and sincerity.

In order to speak with this kind of humility, and in order to speak accurately of God, we need other people. You can't just lock yourself in a room with theology books, read them all, and then suddenly know everything about God. It often takes people who are different from us to enhance our vision of God.

Over dinner one night, I (Tyler) was talking with Emily about the biblical story of Hosea and Gomer. In this story, Hosea, the local holy man, is commanded by God to take Gomer, a prostitute, as his wife. After getting married, Gomer is unfaithful to Hosea. The story is supposed to be an analogy to God's faithful love for Israel and for Israel's lack of faithfulness.

I remarked on how beautiful of a story it is—not even our failings can diminish God's love for us! Emily agreed, but she also helped me see that some details of Hosea were a bit disturbing. For example, Hosea 2 uses language like, "I will strip her naked and expose her as in the day she was born" (v. 3) and "now I will uncover her shame in the sight of her lovers" (v. 10). This imagery of sexual violence and degradation is difficult to read, and Emily pointed out that it should not be glossed over in a quick effort to make the book of Hosea a simple portrait of God's relationship with Israel. We *should* be uncomfortable when we encounter passages like these, and we *should* ask questions—questions like, "How would someone who has survived sexual violence read and experience this passage?"

Emily's favorite Old Testament class at Duke Divinity School, co-taught by a Jewish rabbi named Laura Lieber and an Episcopalian professor named Ellen Davis, had come to Hosea thoughtfully and carefully, reminding Emily and her classmates that any metaphor—pushed too far—has its weaknesses, and while we can find truths in the central metaphor of Hosea, we may want to examine those weaknesses: gender dynamics, power dynamics, etc.

Each person has a distinct vantage point and perspective from which they receive God's revelation. This is simply because each person is different. The places we live, our race, our gender, and our personal experiences all become different perspectives on our lives that affect how we interpret the revelation of God. Even though we all interpret the revelation of God differently, God does not change.

My (Tyler's) friend Tyone, who is a pastor of a Black congregation on Chicago's South Side, helped me understand the theological word "salvation" more clearly. Tyone and I were finishing our seminary education together with an internship as hospital chaplains in a wealthy, predominately white suburb of Chicago. In this meeting with other hospital chaplains (of which Tyone was the only non-white person), white chaplain after white chaplain spoke of God saving us by "taking us to heaven," which they described with ethereal, out-of-this-world adjectives. While it is certainly true that God's salvation extends to an afterlife, it is not the *whole* truth.

Tyone pointed this out to me. While we were walking to our cars, Tyone said, "Did you notice how they all talked about salvation? It's like the only good thing God can do is to take us away from our already-good place and take us to a better place. Well, Tyler, there's more to salvation than that."

Tyone, from his perspective, proceeded to teach me that salvation also happens whenever God steps into the course of history and powerfully works for the good of people—*right here, right now*. Salvation is the mighty power of God magnificently interrupting our lives, he explained.

Tyone told me that considering how I grew up (white, privileged), it would be almost impossible for me to understand this aspect of salvation by myself. It required a dear brother, someone with a different perspective, to help me more fully understand God's salvation.

Without others, our knowledge of God is not necessarily inaccurate—but it is not as full or robust as it could be. As imperfect knowers, our knowledge of God is enhanced and enriched when, with humility, we listen to the insights of our brothers and sisters who can see things of God and of the world that we cannot.

Why?

After reading a chapter about the many ways God is revealed to us, you may be thinking, "But *why* does God go to these lengths to help us understand things?" That's a good, necessary question. It helps us not to "lose the forest in the trees," so to speak.

God reveals God's self to us *because God wants to be known*. Christians proclaim that God's love is excessive, unnecessary. God isn't content to simply love God's own self. God's love continues in the act of giving life to all of creation, and the life God creates is meant for joy. God realizes that without revelation, it is impossible for human beings to see reality, care for others, and love God as we ought. Our lack of knowing is resolved with God's revelation.

God's revelation lets human beings become co-lovers of God, creation, others, and even ourselves. (After all, it's pretty hard to love someone you know nothing about!) God did not create us to sit inside of a cardboard box. God intends for us to be free, to be like God in enjoying God and all that God made. Human life is not designed for ignorant isolation. Revelation is the necessary knowledge given to us by God so we can know and enjoy all that is good.

God does not leave us trapped without knowledge. Through Jesus, the Bible, sacred tradition, and general revelation, God gives us the necessary knowledge to become co-lovers of God. Like a friend who writes letters, sends emails, makes personal phone calls, and visits in person, so too does God devise multiple ways of being known by us. When God's revelation is received with humility—an attentiveness and awareness of God and neighbor—human beings can more fully know and love God.

This chapter has only scratched the surface of the important part of Christian theology that teaches how to be human and what God is like. Jesus, the first way God's revelation comes to us, deserves a whole chapter of his own.

4

The scandal of the Son

Christology

Y ou may have been told at some point that you look like one or both of your parents—you've got your dad's nose, your mom's eyes, the "classic (insert your last name here) ears." It's all part of genetics, all part of being human.

To start off our thinking on Christology—all the things we mean when we talk about Jesus' birth and life and death—let's think about this: Jesus looked like his mom.

Of course, we don't know exactly what Jesus looked like (although we can give you a hint: he wasn't blond!). But we can know a few things, based on the time he lived and where he lived in the world. And because we know he had a human mother, Mary, we can assume he shared a few of her features. Maybe he had her smile, her chin, her tilt of the head. It's all part of being human.

This might sound a little strange, maybe even a bit scandalous: the Son of God having the eyes or hands or ears of a woman from first-century Palestine? Our Lord and Savior looking like another human being? It is a bit strange, and "scandalous" is just the word for this chapter, really. It's the perfect word to describe what's going on when we study who Jesus is, what he did, and what he does today. The word "scandal" shows up a lot when you study theology, because it's part of a phrase scholars use to talk about the mind-boggling reality of Jesus's first-century earthly existence. That phrase is *"the scandal of particularity."*

In this chapter, we'll explore the meaning of that phrase, unpacking its implications for you and for us and for everyone who's ever walked this earth. And we'll talk about how the fact that Jesus looked like his mom means everything.

Defining our terms: a couple councils

Let's begin by flipping the calendar pages back all the way to the year 325 CE.

We've talked about how so much of the task of theology is figuring out what proper God-talk is: How do we describe and speak about God in ways that are true, and not harmful? Much of the groundwork for this task was laid many centuries ago at a couple key *ecumenical councils.* These were gatherings of church leaders, coming together to figure out how to talk about God—because there were people whose God-talk was just a little off. (And by "just a little off," we mean way, way off.)

In 325 CE, the *Council of Nicaea* met to sort through the ways we talk about the relationship between God the Father and God the Son. A teaching called Arianism was in the air, which scoffed at the idea that Jesus was *really* God. "How could God be one being *with* a human being?" Arianism asked. "Sure, Jesus was important—but Jesus had to have been created."

The Council of Nicaea quashed that thought. They declared that Jesus was *not* a created being, but that he and the Father were of one being: *homoousios* in Greek, with *homo* meaning "one" and *ousios* (ou-see-ahs) meaning "substance."

(A quick little story to help you remember what came up at the Council of Nicaea: you know the phrase "not one iota," as in "they didn't get an iota of credit for all their work"? "Iota" is a letter in the Greek alphabet, one that came up in the term the Arians were using to describe the relationship between God the Father and God the Son: *homoiousios,* "of *similar* substance." When it comes to orthodox belief, however, not one iota comes between "one" and "substance" in the Greek: *homoousios!*)

The creed that emerged out of the council at Nicaea—aptly named the *Nicene Creed*—spells out the relationship between Jesus and the Father in a strong rebuke of Arius and his teachings. Jesus is the Son of God and is *begotten* of God, not a created being; Jesus and the Father are one, not two separate beings. And that rebuke is still read out clear in many churches every Sunday:

> We believe in one Lord, Jesus Christ,
> the only Son of God,
> eternally begotten of the Father,
> God from God, Light from Light,
> true God from true God,

begotten, not made,
of one Being with the Father.[1]

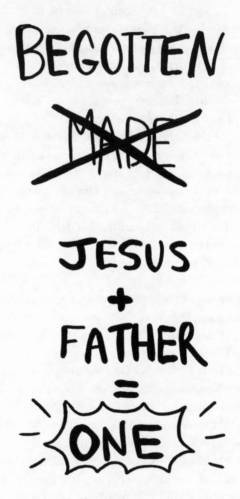

So the Council of Nicaea worked out the Father-Son relationship, but as to how Jesus was both human and divine, we need to flip the calendar forward to the year 451 CE and another ecumenical council: the Council of Chalcedon.

More heresies were in the air. Apollinaris, bishop of Laodicea, taught that Jesus wasn't fully human, like you and me. Eutyches, an abbot in

1. Church of England, "Creed."

Constantinople, taught that Jesus had just one new nature in the incarnation, not a divine and human nature. Nestorius, bishop of Constantinople, taught that Jesus' two natures—his divine nature and human nature—were separable.

The Council of Chalcedon sought to stamp out these ways of describing Jesus and instead speak truly about the wonder of the Word-made-flesh. The Chalcedonian council's concluding statement of faith has come to be known as the Chalcedonian formula. The formula describes Jesus' divine and human natures:

> two natures without confusion, without change, without division, without separation; the distinction of natures being in no way annulled by the union . . .[2]

So Jesus is *both* God *and* human, but his God-ness and his human-ness—while different and distinct—are intertwined and inseparable. The technical phrase used in theological circles for this concept is the *hypostatic union*. And what that union actually *is* is essentially impossible to describe. I (Emily) love how the authors of the *Pocket Dictionary of Theological Terms* define the hypostatic union: "an attempt to describe the miraculous bringing together of humanity and divinity in the same person, Jesus Christ, such that he is both fully divine and fully human."[3] Notice the word "attempt" in there! These formulas and doctrines—even the ones written up by fancy fifth-century church leaders—are all our best human *attempts* at explaining the inexplicable.

One such attempt at explaining this union is through an analogy given by St. Cyril, who was archbishop of Alexandria (and perhaps Nestorius's biggest critic in all these arguments about Jesus). Cyril talked about Jesus' divinity and humanity being like a human being's body and soul.

"Do we not say that a human being like ourselves is one, and has a single nature, even though he is not homogeneous but really composed of two things, I mean soul and body?" he wrote.[4] A person's soul and body are both distinct, but they can't simply be separated from one another. Similarly, "Godhead is one thing, and manhood is another thing," said Cyril, "but in the case of Christ they came together in a mysterious and

2. Bettenson and Maunder, *Documents*, 54.

3. Grenz et al., *Pocket Dictionary*, 62.

4. Saint Cyril, *On the Unity*, 78.

incomprehensible union without confusion or change."[5] But Cyril was well aware that analogies like this—soul-body to divinity-humanity—were just that: *analogies.* Images and illustrations weren't ever going to be enough to explain what was really going on: "the manner of this union is entirely beyond conception."[6]

But now that we've looked at some of the technical terms we use when we talk about Jesus—hypostatic union, *homoousios*—let's get back to our opening observation that Jesus looked like his mom.

What's so scandalous about particularity?

Why does it matter that Jesus looked like his mom? Because when you think about it, all those controversies and councils were trying to figure out how to talk about (and not talk about) that reality. How do we describe the fact that God—the Creator, the Almighty—was born of a woman, took on skin, and walked around with us, and he did it all in a way that didn't compromise God's very own God-ness? But orthodox Christian theology, hammered out across the centuries, says otherwise. Jesus is human, and Jesus is God. As the famous line in John's Gospel goes, "The Word became flesh and lived among us" (1:14). In Jesus, God kneels down to our level.

That in itself—God taking the form of a slave!—is a lot to take in. But here's the thing: in Jesus, God didn't just become anyone. God did not become a Universal Human™, like some kind of blank canvas that we can

5. Saint Cyril, *On the Unity,* 77.
6. Saint Cyril, *On the Unity,* 77.

fill up with all the things that will make God exactly like us. God did not choose to be Anybody in Anywhere.

Instead, God revealed God's own self as a *particular* person in a *particular* place at a *particular* time. The city where Jesus was born? You can find it on a map. The timing of his life? We know what people were eating and drinking back then, how people got around and spoke to each other.

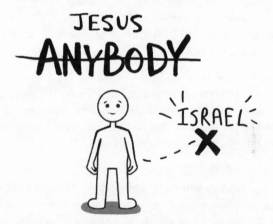

We don't know all the details of Jesus' first-century life, but we know he was a Jewish man living in the Middle East who had brothers and sisters, who worked as a carpenter for a long time. Why a carpenter? Why a man? Why the first century? We don't know. But the person of Jesus is bound to these particulars. Jesus' life cannot be lifted out of his context and squeezed into our own—even though plenty of people have tried to do so.

At first, it might seem like a noble goal to try and do that—aren't we just trying to apply Jesus' first-century teachings to our twenty-first-century lives? Aren't we just trying to figure out how the life of Jesus speaks to our life? There is nothing inherently wrong with those attempts, but what becomes a problem is thinking that Jesus' particularity, his first-century Middle Eastern Jewishness, doesn't really matter that much.

To put it rather bluntly: it is a theological nightmare if Jesus loses his particularity. If Jesus' particularity doesn't matter, then ours doesn't matter. If Jesus is an abstraction, then we are an abstraction. Because Jesus was born to Mary at a specific time and place, because his hair was a certain color and his laugh sounded a certain way, God declared that every detail of our bodies matters because God took them on. The love of God, as Beth Felker Jones reminds us, "is a love that encompasses bodies as well as souls, a love concrete enough to become incarnate, to extend to fingers and toes: both Jesus's and ours. God's love is big enough to love specifics."[7] The *incarnation*—the term we use to describe how "the Word became flesh and lived among us" (John 1:14)—is God's "yes" to pockmarked, smelly, wonderfully made humanity.

But when we forget about that "yes" and all that it entails, our faith can become disembodied and dislocated: something in our heads and not related at all to the place we live or the people around us. The theologian Willie James Jennings writes about how dangerous this is:

> I want Christians to recognize the grotesque nature of a social performance of Christianity that imagines Christian identity floating above land, landscape, animals, place, and space, leaving such realities to the machinations of capitalistic calculations and the commodity chains of private property.[8]

When our faith is "higher than" everything and everyone around us, other gods and masters will creep in below it. We need to remember that our God is a God who walked on earth with us. But this is something we often forget. As Jennings writes, "Christian intellectual tradition in the New World denies its most fundamental starting point, that of the divine Word entering flesh in time and space to become Jewish flesh."[9]

7. Jones, *Practicing Christian Doctrine*, 137.

8. Jennings, *Christian Imagination*, 293.

9. Jennings, *Christian Imagination*, 113.

That leads to something else we need to explore. We need to talk about one aspect of Jesus' particularity that tends to be tossed aside more than all the others (and the theological nightmare of doing that): his *Jewishness*. It's almost like a lot of Christians look at Jesus and see him as "the first Christian," discarding the fact of his Jewish faith because they are not Jews. Jesus, however, was not just a practicing Jew—he is described as "the true Israelite," the fulfillment of Israel. Scholars will talk about the "threefold office," the *munus triplex*, of Jesus: Christ as prophet, priest, and king; as a sort of bridge between the Old and New Testaments, Jesus is the new Elijah, Aaron, and David.[10] But being the "new" Elijah, Aaron, and David does not mean the original Elijah, Aaron, and David have no purpose anymore— that because of Jesus, we don't have to pay attention to the story of Israel, or that we can look at the Old Testament and simply plug in "the church" or "Christians" whenever we see references to Israel and the Jewish people. (Not-so-fun fact: this is called *supersessionism*, and it is real, and it is every- where!) Instead, gentile believers in Jesus (and most believers in Jesus are now gentiles) are now part of Israel's story too, because the work of Jesus has grafted us onto it, like a branch being lovingly and carefully grafted onto a tree. But, wittingly or unwittingly, many, many Christians—particularly white Western Christians—have believed themselves and their churches to be the "replacement" for Israel and have tried to divorce Jesus from his Jewishness, with disastrous results for actual Jewish people.

Jennings, in his book *The Christian Imagination*, talks about Jesus' Jewishness—and what it means for us—in this way:

> The story of Jesus never leaves Israel. This is not the denial of the universality of Jesus' life. However, universality . . . is a highly dan- gerous concept that, bound to the legacies of supersessionism and whiteness, did and continues to do strange things to the story of Jesus. I suggest a commitment not to an abstract idea of the uni- versal or even of the universal applicability of Jesus, but to follow Jesus' own trajectory toward the many in Israel and through Israel to the many in the world.[11]

Jennings warns us about what can happen when we try to make Jesus "universal": the dangers of trying to replace Israel with the church, of mak- ing Jesus blond-haired and blue-eyed. Jennings instead offers us another

10. Wright, *Knowing Jesus*, 2.
11. Jennings, *Christian Imagination*, 265.

way forward, the one that Jesus himself walked: of opening his arms to the people of Israel and, through them, to the whole world.

How particularity saves us

We've seen how Jesus' particularity proclaims the importance of our own particularity, and how it shows our connection to the story of God's work with Israel. But Jesus' particularity does even more than this. It's how he is able to save us.

Because Jesus wasn't just a "generic person" but rather a *particular* person in space and time, who can "sympathize with our weaknesses . . . who in every respect has been tested as we are" (Heb 4:15), he is able to redeem every aspect of our human experience. Some of the early church fathers talked about this, saying how "only what has been endured is healed and saved."[12] In order for us to be healed and saved, Jesus had to become like us—particular people in particular times. We are not abstractions—and Jesus wasn't either.

On the wood of a Roman cross, Jesus didn't get to skip through any of the suffering of human death because he was God. He lived and he died as one of us, with all of the specific suffering that entails. The theologian Hans Urs von Balthasar writes about how important it is to recognize "the solidarity of the Crucified with all the human dead."[13] But it's not just solidarity in the sense of knowing and understanding—it's solidarity that *saves* us. Remember what all those councils declared? Jesus was fully human *and* fully God. And in his fully human experience of death, he—God the Son—conquered it.

I (Emily) love to read these lines from Balthasar and imagine Jesus walking to the limits of death and suffering, standing at the edge, and decreeing that none of us ever have to do what he did:

> It is *he* who sets the limits to the extension of damnation, who forms the boundary stone marking the place where the lowest pitch is reached and the reverse movement set into operation. . . . The Redeemer showed himself therefore as the only one who, going beyond the general experience of death, was able to measure the depths of that abyss.[14]

12. Balthasar, *Mysterium Paschale*, 165.
13. Balthasar, *Mysterium Paschale*, 160.
14. Balthasar, *Mysterium Paschale*, 167, 168.

Jesus—who became like us in every way—bled and died as a human being so that we never have to taste the kind of suffering he faced.

Particularity as a permanent choice

Of course, you probably know the Easter story, and you probably know that Jesus' death is not how this story ends. It's also not how the story of God's choice to become like us ends.

In John 20, Jesus appears to Thomas after his resurrection and shows him the marks in his hands and side.

> A week later his disciples were again in the house, and Thomas was with them. Although the doors were shut, Jesus came and stood among them and said, "Peace be with you." Then he said to Thomas, "Put your finger here and see my hands. Reach out your hand and put it in my side. Do not doubt but believe." (vv. 26–27)

It says something that Jesus' skin wasn't just magically smooth and healed up once he had returned from the dead. It tells us that the body Jesus had is the one he had chosen to be in for good. The incarnation is God's *permanent* choice.

And that's amazing news for you and me and everyone: God loves us enough to become like us forever.

Jesus still had the scars of the crucifixion when he was with Thomas, but maybe it seems like he would decide to do away with them once he ascended into heaven. But a good theology of Jesus' ascension means we don't simply do away with our bodies. (More on that in the chapter on *eschatology*!) Jesus' body was clearly different after his resurrection (note his ability to enter a room "although the doors were shut"), but his wounds did not disappear—and right now, at the right hand of the Father, Jesus still bears the marks of those wounds as he speaks words of love on our behalf. As Beth Felker Jones writes, "[Jesus'] humanity did not end with the ascension. The ascension means that he has become one of us for keeps, that he represents our humanity, right now, today, to the Father."[15]

We'll leave you with a note on Jesus' scars from the priest, professor, and author Barbara Brown Taylor:

> [Jesus] wanted them to know he had gone through the danger and not around it, so he told them to look—not at his face, not into his eyes—but at his hands and feet, which told the truth about what had happened to him, which were the only proof he had that he was who he said he was. Some of us wish he had come back all cleaned up, but he did not. He left us something to recognize him by—his hands and feet, just like ours, or almost like ours. You know what his said about him. What do ours say about us? Where have they been, whom have they touched, how have they served, what have they proclaimed?[16]

And on that note: now that we know a bit more about how God chose to become like us, we can take a look at how we show the world what God is like. How? By becoming "little images" of God.

---

15. Jones, *Practicing Christian Doctrine*, 188.
16. Taylor, *Home by Another Way*, 122–23.

5

Why are we here?

Theological anthropology

A t some point, we all wonder: "What is the purpose of my life?" This question is pretty deep and complex, but Christian theology gives a really clear answer: the purpose of human life is *to be a small image of God's life*. But how Christians arrived at this answer (and what it means for you and me) requires a bit more of an explanation—and some drawings, too.

Tselem

We've settled on this definition of the purpose of human life because that is how the Bible describes it. (Remember the chapter about revelation?)

In the book of Genesis, the first book of the Bible, the author recounts the creation of the world. At the end of the creation process, on the sixth day, God created human beings. At this point, the writer makes a theological point and notes, "So God created humans in his image, in the image of God he created them; male and female he created them" (Gen 1:27).

God created us in God's *image*. This word is really important—hang with us for a bit of a detour into the realm of ancient Near Eastern religion. The fact that we are made in God's *image* is the key to understanding our purpose as human beings.

The word in our English Bibles for "image" is translated from the Hebrew word *tselem*, which literally means "idol." As a matter of fact, the Hebrew word *tselem*—or rather, its equivalents in the various languages of the ancient Near East—was common in the religious vocabulary of the nations that neighbored ancient Israel, such as Assyria, Egypt, and Phoenicia. For Israel's neighbors, the worship of their gods often required them to create a *tselem* to represent their god. These worshippers certainly didn't think that the *tselem* (the idol or image) of their god was *actually* the god itself. They believed that the *tselem* was a visual representation of what their god was like. If ancient worshippers wanted to know what their god was like, all they had to do was worship at the *tselem* of a particular god.

Now this is when things get interesting—and we mean *really* interesting.

When the writers of the Bible note that we are made in God's image, or *tselem*, they are saying that God has chosen for us to be his representatives. Another way to say it goes like this: *God wants people to see what divine life is like when they look at human life.*

Your life, when rightly lived, can show other people what God is like.

This is why God asks us, multiple times, to not create or fashion or cast idols. God doesn't want us to make idols that represent him because *we ourselves* already are God's representatives!

The purpose of human life is found in this profound fact of our creation. The purpose of our life isn't really about us: instead, it is to show what God's life is like in how we think, speak, dream, and act.

This picture is helpful in understanding that our purpose in life is to show God's life:

This person—bearing the image of God—still is a human, with unique facial features, personality traits, and all that comes with being a person. But, when you look at them, you can also see that small drawing we've been using for God. When you look at this person, you see both them *and* God.

In God's kindness, God made each of us with tenderness and purpose. We are not mistakes. Every single person is of incomparable worth and dignity, simply because of this theological truth: that we are created in the image of God. Regardless of skills, abilities, wealth, poverty, gender, or religious affiliation, every single person is created in the image of God.

Since every person is made in the image of God, with the infinite worth and dignity that comes with it, this theological truth informs how we are to treat others. For instance, people are not their professions. Doctors or lawyers or wealthy business people do not require particular adoration. They are people made in the image of God—people with value and meaning simply because God wants them to be. People who work in service jobs do not exist merely to serve others; they exist to be an image of God. It is a theological nightmare to treat people differently based upon their profession.

The scholar and author C. S. Lewis wrote the following in his sermon titled "The Weight of Glory":

> It is a serious thing to live in a society of possible gods and goddesses, to remember that the dullest and most uninteresting person you talk to may one day be a creature which, if you saw it now, you would be strongly tempted to worship, or else a horror and a corruption such as you now meet, if at all, only in a nightmare. All day long we are, in some degree, helping each other to one or other of these destinations. It is in the light of these overwhelming possibilities, it is with the awe and the circumspection proper to them, that we should conduct all our dealings with one another, all friendships, all loves, all play, all politics. There are no *ordinary* people. You have never talked to a mere mortal. . . . Next to the Blessed Sacrament itself, your neighbour is the holiest object presented to your senses.[1]

When humans faithfully and actively bear God's image, it means that when other people see them, they see glimmers of God. Human beings have the wonderful privilege to be small images of God to others. This is what we were made for.

---

1. Lewis, *Weight of Glory*, 45–46.

Since our lives are meant to show what God's life is like, it is *extremely* important that we understand what God is like.

What is God like?

We've already learned a good deal about what God is like in the earlier chapters. God *loves*—eternally existing as Father, Son, and Spirit. God *creates*—extending life and love to that which is separate from God. God *reveals*—graciously granting us the necessary knowledge to become co-lovers of God. But maybe the most succinct way to describe God is to say that *God takes great joy in others.*

God delights in this world and in us. These words of Jesus are recorded in Matthew:

> Look at the birds of the air: they neither sow nor reap nor gather into barns, and yet your heavenly Father feeds them. . . . Consider the lilies of the field, how they grow; they neither toil nor spin, yet I tell you, even Solomon in all his glory was not clothed like one of these. (6:26a, 28b–29)

If there was any doubt that Jesus was simply speaking metaphorically, he explicitly states in John 3 that "God so loved the world." And this joy God takes in creation extends to human beings, too. Marveling at God's kindness to humanity, the psalmist proclaims in Psalm 8:4–5, "What are humans that you are mindful of them, mortals that you care for them? Yet you have made them a little lower than God and crowned them with glory and honor." With love and affection, God chooses to sustain all of reality in every moment simply because *it pleases God*. If God chose to not constantly uphold creation, we might all become nothing. As Karl Barth wrote, "Our existence can be understood only as an event of inconceivable kindness, or it cannot be understood at all."[2]

A few years ago, I (Tyler) was visiting my sister and her son, my nephew Henry, who was two at the time. My sister asked if I wanted to wake him up from his afternoon nap. Any time spent with Henry is delightful, and I scooped him up from his crib and brought him downstairs. Still groggy, he asked to sit on the couch and have a story read to him. I grabbed his favorite book (which he affectionately calls "The Cars Book") and read. Henry

---

2. Barth, *CD* 1/1:444.

snuggled next to me and rested his head on my chest. While I read, I could tell he was looking up at me, so I asked, "Henry, how are you, my friend?"

"I'm just so happy," he replied.

"Why?"

"Because I just love you so much."

This is a glimpse into the love God has for us. "I'm just so happy. . . . I just love you so much." These words express the great joy God takes in us and in all of creation.

If God takes great joy in us (which God does), and if we are to be small images of what God is like (which we are), then this opens up nearly infinite possibilities of how we can bear the image of God and realize our purpose in life. Pursuing our purpose in life doesn't limit our lives into a tight box of what career we must pursue or what personality traits we should have. Bearing the image of God does just the opposite—it encourages us to show others what God is like simply by doing ordinary things with extraordinary joy.

Tending your garden? This can show the world that God takes great joy in small things like soils that sustain life. Changing the diaper of a grumpy, impossible-to-pin-down baby? This can show the world that God takes great joy in giving what is best for us, even when we resist. Attending a city council meeting to speak up for the rights of immigrants in your neighborhood? This can show the world that God cares for the oppressed. Fulfilling our purpose in life does not mean that we all have to be or act the same—you weren't created in a factory to be just like everyone else. Bearing God's image is as simple as allowing the particularities and details of our life to be brush strokes on the greater picture that shows others what God is like.

When human beings take great joy in God's creation, they show others a glimpse of the God who takes great joy in God's creation. According to Christian theology, that is what humans were created to do.

Avoiding toxic theology

We have to be careful about all of this, too. The good news that we can show the world what God is like can become toxic if we aren't careful.

Bearing God's image means that our purpose is to be *like* God, not to *be* God. Theology can become toxic if we put too much pressure on ourselves to change the world, to be perfect, and to be just like God. The good news is that Jesus already changed the world—so we simply bear witness to God's power with our contentment and faithfulness.

Also, it is toxic to believe that bearing God's image means that every single Christian is supposed to bear God's image in the same way. Bearing God's image doesn't make our preferences or personalities irrelevant.

When I (Tyler) was a teenager, I was insecure. (I know: unique, right?) I was, and still am, quite small, less physically strong than other men. I was, and still am, very talkative. Growing up, I thought the ideal Christian man was tall, broad-shouldered, not sensitive, and not talkative. Sometimes I thought I needed to change who I was so I would fit into the image of what an "ideal Christian man" was.

Thankfully, I have a loving dad who took the time to understand my insecurities, and in doing so, he also corrected my toxic theology. With my doubts and insecurities, my dad always tells me that "God doesn't make mistakes—and God didn't make one when he made you, either."

By reminding me that God didn't make a mistake when he made me small or when he made me talkative, my dad helped me to take my insecure eyes off the people I compared myself to around me. He helped me fix my eyes on God, the one whose image I get to bear.

As much as I wish I could always have my dad around to give me these pep talks, that's not realistic. (Or developmentally appropriate.) But one thing I can do every single week to avoid the toxic theology of comparing myself to other "ideal Christian men" is to worship with others at my local church.

I have a favorite part of weekly worship, called the fraction. During this part of the worship service, our pastor takes the communion wafer and holds it high above her head. This forces me to physically lift my head and gaze up, but figuratively to pull my eyes away from anything other than God that I am tempted to imitate.

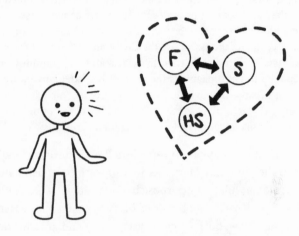

Our pastor then takes the wafer and physically breaks it in two, saying, "Christ our Passover Lamb has been sacrificed, once and for all upon the cross." This is a physical reminder that God is the One who loves us to the point of death; in dying, God proves there is nothing he would not do to show the depth of his love for us. Likewise, my life is to be broken in love for the world. Every single week, by worshiping in my local church, I see that the image of God I am called to bear, the purpose of my life, is to offer myself in love for others, just like Jesus did for me.

Our purpose in life is to bear God's image, not the image of those we deem "ideal."

Mary

Bearing God's image doesn't mean there is a single way we must act. Instead, it opens up nearly infinite possibilities of how our seemingly daily and mundane acts, done with remarkable joy, can be a small image of what

God is like. Sometimes that can feel a bit overwhelming—like, where do we start? I think a flesh-and-blood example of someone who faithfully bore God's image can be a good starting point.

Jesus' mom, Mary, is a role model who shows us our purpose as human beings. (After all, she literally carried God around in her womb for nine months.)

Professor and author Abigail Rine Favale writes,

> Mary gives us a picture of a human soul so completely united to God that she becomes translucent; she shows us not herself, but God within her, the Word becoming flesh for our sake. In her person, she displays the essence of the Christian life—a creature who gives herself in complete trust to her Creator. Her humility and receptivity to God magnifies the scale of his redemptive work— the vast expanse he traverses to draw near to us, to pitch his tent among us. Mary, full of grace, exhibits a restoration of the *imago Dei*, the divine image etched upon the human creature.[3]

Even though you and I aren't capable of literally bearing God's flesh in our bodies in the same way Mary did, we can learn from her. By following her example, we can fulfill our purpose in life of showing God's life.

First, and perhaps most obviously, Mary loves and adores God. Mary held Jesus in her arms, both when he was a baby and after his death. She treasured up in her heart the moments of Jesus' growing-up years. She faithfully accompanied Jesus throughout his earthly ministry. To Mary, Jesus was to be adored, enjoyed. She didn't take his life or presence for granted. One of the many ways we can bear God's image is to take great joy in God, and in doing so, show the world that God takes great joy in us. A priest once advised Favale "to draw close to Mary, to learn how to better love her Son."[4] We can do the same.

Mary is also humble. She chooses to respond to suffering with faithfulness. After Mary is told by the angel Gabriel that she—a young virgin—will conceive and bear a son, she responds by saying, "Here am I, the servant of the Lord; let it be with me according to your word" (Luke 1:38). In being the mother of Jesus, Mary had to endure the shameful glances by people who assumed the worst of Jesus' conception, an exile to Egypt, and later, possibly the most painful thing a human being can experience: watching her child die. In all of this, Mary is humble; she chooses to bear

3. Favale, *Into the Deep*, 164.
4. Favale, *Into the Deep*, 138.

patiently with her suffering. As human beings, we are all called to suffer. Even Jesus suffered. Mary's response to her impending suffering—saying, "Let it be with me according to your word"—is reminiscent of how her son chooses to respond to his Father right before his hour of suffering, in John 12:27–28a: "Now my soul is troubled. And what should I say: 'Father, save me from this hour'? No, it is for this reason that I have come to this hour. Father, glorify your name." Mary and her son are both willing to let their inevitable suffering be used as a small image of the God who willingly suffers in order to display the extent of his love.

Mary is full of gratitude and praise. While pregnant with Jesus, she praises God. Her prayer is so beautiful, I will quote it in its entirety:

> My soul magnifies the Lord,
>> and my spirit rejoices in God my Savior,
>> for he has looked with favor on the lowly state of his servant.
>>> Surely from now on all generations will call me blessed,
>> for the Mighty One has done great things for me,
>> and holy is his name;
> indeed, his mercy is for those who fear him
>> from generation to generation.
> He has shown strength with his arm;
>> he has scattered the proud in the imagination of their hearts.
> He has brought down the powerful from their thrones
>> and lifted up the lowly;
> he has filled the hungry with good things
>> and sent the rich away empty.
> He has come to the aid of his child Israel,
>> in remembrance of his mercy,
> according to the promise he made to our ancestors,
>> to Abraham and to his descendants forever. (Luke 1:46–55)

By responding to God with praise and adoration, Mary shows us that when human life is properly lived, we lift our gaze upward, praising God, directing attention and honor away from ourselves and toward God.

But after reading this, be careful to not think that Mary is simply a polite, grateful woman. She is a woman of conscience and justice. When Mary and her husband present the baby Jesus in the temple, they offer a sacrifice of two small pigeons. Usually, when a baby was presented in the temple, a lamb or sheep was sacrificed. Pigeons were reserved for those who, in their poverty, could not afford anything bigger. Mary knew firsthand the harmful effects of poverty and injustice. In her adoration of God, she says, "He has brought down the powerful from their thrones and lifted up the lowly; he has filled the hungry with good things and sent the rich away empty." Mary does not approve (and neither does God!) of the unjust systems that operate in our world, a world in which some gorge themselves in pride while others starve.

The example of Mary, the God-bearer, asks the question one of my professors, Matt Milliner, often asked us students: "Has Christ been born of me today?"

The purpose of our lives is to reflect God's life, and luckily for us, our God became a human. Both Jesus and his mother give us concrete ways of living that help us show the world what God is like.

According to Christian theology, the purpose of human life is not to be successful, gain wealth or influence, or even to change the world. Our purpose is far simpler and greater: to live our lives as small images of divine life. This means that everything we say, do, and think is loaded with potential—the potential to bless others and the world around us.

Unfortunately, however, our lives and our world are filled with the tragic reality of the consequences that come when human beings reject their purpose in life. This rejection of God—sin—will be the focus of our next chapter.

6

Missing the mark

Hamartiology

As we've seen, the purpose of human life is to be a small image of God's life. When we live in accordance with God's ways, we give the world a small sampling of what God is like. Sadly—and does this really have to be said explicitly?—human beings fall short of our calling to be images of God, time and time again. Theologically speaking, Christians call this failure to live up to our calling *sin*, and the study of sin is called *hamartiology* (we'll unpack that term a little later).

Sin isn't as simple as doing something wrong. It's actually a whole state of being that is askew. Trapped in a state of sin, people selfishly turn in on themselves. Curved inward, seeing just themselves and ignoring the world they were made to love, sinful human beings reject their purpose in life. Human beings are called to show others the love of God, who is for others. But sin is a state of selfishly seeking our own good, not the good of others.

Sin, unfortunately, isn't an abstract philosophical thing. It has real-world consequences, and it harms our relationship with others and the world.

Incurvatus in se

When human beings sin, rejecting their calling to be like God, their life looks a little bit like this:

This person is trapped in a state of sin. Their back curves inward as they focus on themselves. In the previous chapter, we saw a drawing of a person bearing the image of God—but in this person, you cannot see any glimmers of God.

German theologian Martin Luther describes humans in a state of sin as *incurvatus in se*, which is Latin for "curved inward on oneself." (It's also worth noting that this idea wasn't original to Luther; Augustine first wrote about it a thousand years prior.) Elaborating on this, Luther writes, "Scripture describes man as so curved in upon himself that he uses not only physical but even spiritual goods for his own purposes and in all things seeks only himself."[1]

Luther describes sin as a tragic, consequence-laden state for human beings. The important phrase here is *"in all things seeks only himself."* Seeking only themselves when in a state of sin, human beings fail to take great joy in others. As we read in the chapter on human anthropology, God takes great joy in us, and we are happiest when we take great joy in others and in the world around us. In a state of sin, humans are too self-focused to take great joy in either.

The calling of human beings is to be small images of God. Theologically speaking, the exact opposite of this is to cave inward, and *not* show others what God is like. When this happens, human beings rupture the bond of love that is meant to keep us in friendship with God and one another.

1. Luther, *Lectures*, 345.

Sin harms

As we mentioned earlier, sin is not just an idea we study: it has real, everyday effects. Not only does sin deprive us of our God-given purpose, but through it we also inflict harm on ourselves, others, and all of creation.

It can be easy to forget this if you think of sin as a matter of following the right rules: "Do this; do that. Don't do this; don't do that."

In Christian theology, we must consistently reject the idea that we can avoid sin simply by following a list of rules. Sin is not the inability to live up to some moral code—it is the self caved inward, unable to love others as it should.

When reflecting on her childhood belief that sin was primarily about breaking rules, Abigail Rine Favale writes:

> I did not see sin as a kind of self-poisoning, partaking of something inherently bad for me. Rather, sin was wrong primarily because it violated the mandates of Scripture, or the norms of the community. In other words, all sin could be distilled down to one underlying infraction: disobedience. This introduced a subtly arbitrary character to sin; I could know a particular action was bad, because the Bible said so, but I didn't have a deeper sense of *why*.[2]

When human beings sin, real people get hurt. Telling a lie is not sinful because there is a rule that says we should tell the truth. Lying is sinful because it *harms* others. It destroys trust. It causes distrust and division where there should instead be unity. Greed is sinful not because we are supposed to follow the Christian tradition of giving away 10 percent of what we have. Greed is sinful because it harms those around us: in a world of abundance, it is wrong to hoard your assets while ignoring your neighbors.

Sin also causes harm to ourselves. We are meant to grow in love, to be like God, and sin stunts our development as people. For example, becoming bitter and failing to forgive others harms us. Writer Anne Lamott describes the failure to forgive and nursing a grudge as "drinking rat poison and then waiting for the rat to die."[3]

When we fail to forgive those who have sinned against us, we grow bitter. The wound that someone inflicted upon us festers and worsens. When we choose to not forgive, we choose not to live in love. There's a reason that when Jesus teaches us to pray in Matthew 6, he instructs us to

2. Favale, *Into the Deep*, 127.
3. Lamott, *Traveling Mercies*, 134.

ask for forgiveness from our heavenly Father for ourselves, and also for the courage to forgive those who sin against us:

> And forgive us our debts,
> as we also have forgiven our debtors. (v. 12)

Jesus is well aware—and wants to make sure we understand—that sin is a harmful, toxic poison that harms us and harms others.

Sin harms others

When humans are turned inward on themselves, they fail to accurately see their neighbors. Other human beings are an occasion to marvel at God's wonderful creation. But in a state of sin, we can't fully see the goodness in one another. German theologian Dietrich Bonhoeffer writes,

> God did not make this person as I would have made him. He did not give him to me as a brother for me to dominate and control, but in order that I might find above him the Creator. Now the other person, in the freedom with which he was created, becomes the occasion of joy, whereas before he was only a nuisance and an affliction. God does not will that I should fashion the other person according to the image that seems good to me, that is, in my own image; rather in his very freedom from me God made this person in His image. I can never know beforehand how God's image should appear in others. That image always manifests a completely new and unique form that comes solely from God's free and sovereign creation. To me the sight may seem strange, even ungodly. But God creates every man in the likeness of His Son, the Crucified. After all, even that image certainly looked strange and ungodly to me before I grasped it.
>
> Strong and weak, wise and foolish, gifted or ungifted, pious or impious, the diverse individuals in the community, are no longer incentives for talking and judging and condemning, and thus excuses for self-justification. They are rather cause for rejoicing in one another and serving one another.[4]

In this lengthy (sorry!) quotation, Bonhoeffer summarizes that in a sinful state, we judge and criticize others. But when we are faithfully bearing God's image, our proper response to others is to be attentive

---

4. Bonhoeffer, *Life Together*, 93.

toward them, to respect and love them. Sin, however, destroys our ability to properly see one another.

With our failure to see others properly when we are in a state of sin, we reduce and shrink them. To be in healthy relationships with others, we have to listen to others, to learn what makes them tick.

A good friend and mentor of mine named Steve pointed out a really interesting phrase the apostle Paul uses in his Letter to the Philippians. Paul loves the church there so much, and he remarks, "I hold you in my heart" (1:7). Instead of being sinful and shrinking people to fit inside of his heart, Paul chooses to *expand* the size of his heart, so that people—with all their quirks and eccentricities—can live there. But in a state of sin, we fail to expand our hearts. We shrink them instead.

In our selfishness, we perceive minor differences of preference as value judgments about the worth of other human beings. "Oh my gosh, can you believe that they don't wake up until 8:30? They must be so lazy," says the morning person who consumes three cups of coffee and checks a litany of items off their to-do list by 6:30 a.m.

Other people are complex, beautiful. But in a state of sin, we fail to see others as precious. Turned inward on ourselves, we fail to celebrate others as we should.

Sin harms our relationship with creation

Sin stains everything—and that means *everything*, more than just our relationships with other people and with ourselves. We see this in the story that theologians have dubbed "the fall," which you maybe heard about in a Sunday School class with a flannel board.

In the beginning, God created a garden and placed two people there, Adam and Eve. God told them to tend and care for and enjoy all that he gave them. There was only one caveat: some knowledge for them was a bit too wonderful, so God asked that they refrain from eating from a particular tree. And, you guessed it—they ate from that tree. Chaos ensued—not just for Adam and Eve, but for all that God made. Look at this drawing:

Here we see the first human being, Adam, sitting *incurvatus in se* outside of the garden of Eden—that perfect paradise where we were created to live in love with everything and everyone. Adam is facing the other way, unable to enjoy the goodness of all that God gave him. That's because this state of sin doesn't just harm Adam and Eve—it harms everything around them, too.

The birds that once sang in the morning to wake Adam up no longer do so. The soil that once gave birth to delicious food and beautiful plants now requires harsh toil and labor. The sun that could warm his skin now burns it. Sin harms everything.

Theologians often call this "total depravity," meaning that *everything* in creation is stained by this state of sin. Everything is poisoned.

Peruvian priest and theologian Gustavo Gutiérrez writes, "Sin is not considered as an individual, private, or merely interior reality. . . . Sin is evident in oppressive structures, in the exploitation of humans by humans, in the domination and slavery of peoples, races, and social classes. Sin appears, therefore, as the fundamental alienation, the root of a situation of injustice and exploitation."[5]

Gutiérrez's point is incredibly important. Sin doesn't just have private consequences for us human beings in our personal relationships with family and friends—it has global, even cosmic, consequences.

In this sense, sin might be the easiest of all doctrines to prove. Our global problems—like war, racism, and environmental degradation—betray humanity's sinful state. We are the ones who have started these problems. And human history—replete with genocide, atomic bombs, and slave trades—could, in the words of Marilynne Robinson, "make a stone weep."[6]

Sin—our selfish inability to be for others—stains our families, economies, governments, and environment. Curved in on themselves in selfishness, human beings can cause great harm to the world around them.

Conclusion

If misunderstood, the doctrine of sin can be harmful in two primary ways.

First, if we think of sin as simply breaking a moral code, we are bound to hurt other people. When we sin, in our failure to be for others, we harm others. When we sin, we must be humble. We must apologize. Sin severs

5. Gutiérrez, *Theology of Liberation*, 103.
6. Robinson, *Gilead*, 225.

the bonds between people, and repairing those bonds requires humility and kindness. We must make restitution to those we have harmed. We have to rebuild trust, which often takes time.

And since sin also harms ourselves, we must critically reflect, too. We have to ask ourselves hard questions like, "Why was I selfish? What held me back from showing the love I should have?" If sin is a state (which it is!), then we must be wise, introspective.

Second, it can be harmful if we allow sin to drive us to unhealthy levels of shame. Sin does not make human beings worthless. It's helpful to know that when the New Testament writers describe sin, they use the Greek word *hamartolos*, which is actually an archery term, used to describe when someone shoots an arrow, but misses the mark.

Missing the mark is a helpful metaphor for understanding sin (and *hamartolos* is where we get the term "hamartiology"!). When an archer misses a shot, they don't put their bow and arrow down and never try again. Likewise, when we notice ourselves not being for others, it shouldn't drive us to so much shame that we give up.

When I (Tyler) was in college, there were a couple of people who upset me. I felt slighted. When I was talking on the phone with my grandma a week after that frustrating encounter, I told her about it, complaining about how others treated me. I wanted her to join in my pity party, to say some bad things about those other people. But she didn't. She was gracious and calmly said, "It sounds like they are simply doing the best they know how."

My grandma understood that sometimes people miss the mark. You and I are prone to curving in on ourselves and being selfish. But when we notice ourselves in a state of sin, the solution isn't to berate ourselves or others. We should treat ourselves with the same kindness that God treats us with, trusting that over time, the Holy Spirit will straighten our spiritual posture and help us to live in love toward the entire world.

But we don't turn away from our sinful state toward a loving state simply by gritting our teeth and trying harder. Instead, for Christians, we accept with gratitude the gift of the Holy Spirit, the Third Person of the Trinity, who helps us grow in love.

7

Speaking of the Spirit

Pneumatology

T he Holy Spirit is not a bird.

Remember back in the Trinity chapter, when we talked about how Jesus' baptism provides a wonderful image of trinitarian life? Here's how the Spirit is described in that scene:

> And when Jesus had been baptized, just as he came up from the water, suddenly the heavens were opened to him and he saw God's Spirit descending like a dove and alighting on him. (Matt 3:16)

Notice: God's Spirit descends *like* a dove. The Spirit is *not* a dove. Or wind, or water, or fire, or any of the other images that are often used to illustrate the Spirit.

But if you grew up in the church, when you think "Holy Spirit," you might picture a dove or wind or flames, because the Spirit is kind of hard to describe—and a lot of times, the Spirit isn't described at all.

In many churches, the Spirit is often the overlooked person of the Trinity: you might hear a *lot* about God the Father and God the Son, but the Spirit makes only occasional appearances in the sermons and songs. And when we *do* talk about the Spirit, we often have to resort to metaphors and images that get at what we're trying to say. Barbara Brown Taylor describes this conundrum so well:

> Of all the persons of the Trinity, I suppose the Holy Spirit is the hardest to define. Most of us can at least begin to describe the other two: God the Father, creator of heaven and earth, who makes the sun shine and the rain fall. God the Son, who was human like us: our savior, teacher, helper, and friend. But how would you describe God the Holy Spirit to a five-year-old child? Even Jesus had a hard time with that one. "The Spirit blows where it chooses," he said in John's gospel, "and you hear the sound of it, but you do not know where it comes from or where it goes" (3:8).[1]

As Taylor notes, Jesus' description of the Spirit hints at the mystery and the unknowns that are always present in our study of the Spirit. The technical term for that study is *pneumatology*. Why call it "pneumatology"? The Greek word *pneuma* means "spirit"—hence "pneumatology" as "Spirit study." Even though there is so much about the work of the Spirit that we cannot fully grasp (as is the case with so much theology!), we can still make some important claims about who the Spirit is and what the Spirit does. Think back to the Nicene Creed, which tells us that Jesus was "conceived by the Holy Spirit and born of the Virgin Mary." The Creed tells us a few other key things—that the Spirit is "the Lord, the giver of life, who proceeds from the Father and the Son, who with the Father and the Son is worshipped and glorified, who has spoken through the prophets."[2]

These few short phrases contain volumes about the Spirit and have much to teach us. In this chapter, we'll introduce some of the ideas that are talked about in pneumatology. We'll do that by drawing a couple pictures that shine a little light on different aspects of the Spirit's work, aspects that are seen in those lines from the Creed: the Spirit as a person of the Trinity, and the Spirit as a helper and healer in the world.

---

1. Taylor, *Home by Another Way*, 145.
2. Church of England, "Creed."

"With the Father and the Son": the immanent Trinity

When we talk about the Spirit, we talk about the Third Person of the Trinity. Like we said in the Trinity chapter, it's important to talk about the members of the Trinity as "persons" instead of "parts" or "pieces"—remembering, however, that they are not "people" in the creaturely sense, with separate minds or wills.

And when we talk about the Spirit's relationship with the other two persons of the Trinity, we first talk about an embrace, a bond of love between them. (Remember *perichoresis*, that dynamic dance of love and joy within the Trinity?)

We also say that, as God, the Spirit is *not made*. And, unlike the Son, the Spirit is not begotten. Rather, we say that the Spirit *proceeds* from the Father (and the Son, in Western theology—more on that in a minute). This "processions" term is what we use when we talk about the relationships between the persons of the Trinity. If we want to get even more technical, we say that the Father *spirates* the Spirit, just as he begets the Son. (Side note: "spirate" is a great word, and we should use it more often—which means we'll be talking about the Spirit more often. Win, win.)

At this point in the book, though, you could probably guess that these terms and doctrines of the Spirit were not agreed on in peace and harmony—and you would be right. In fact, statements about the Spirit played a role in one of the biggest splits in church history.

The original Nicene Creed stated that the Spirit proceeded "from the Father," and only from the Father. But that would change. Leaders in the Western church were concerned with "reaffirming the full divinity of both Spirit and Son in their eternal relationships to one another."[3] They would eventually change that line of the Nicene Creed to read that the Spirit "proceeds from the Father *and the Son*." The Western church leaders spoke Latin, and the Latin term for "and the Son" is *filioque*—and the Eastern church still does not recognize it as part of the Creed. Greek-speaking church leaders in the East believed that claiming the Spirit proceeding from both Father and Son lessened the Spirit's significance. They also did not appreciate the fact that they weren't included in the major decision to add the *filioque* to the Creed. Ultimately, the Eastern and Western churches would break apart in 1054 CE, with the *filioque* as one of the key reasons.

Thinking on the *filioque*, and all the other aspects of the Spirit's relationship with the Father and Son, is part of what we talked about back in the creation chapter as the *immanent Trinity* perspective: the inner

3. Jones, *Practicing Christian Doctrine*, 171.

movement and workings of the Godhead. But you might remember that there's another term—the *economic Trinity*—to talk about the relationships of the Trinity with that which is not God. And when the Spirit blows and breezes into creation, some wild things start to happen.

"He has spoken through the prophets": the economic Trinity

When we consider the economic Trinity perspective, we consider what the persons of the Trinity are doing in the world. The Spirit works wonders in the world in countless ways, and one of the chief ways we talk about that work is through a name Jesus used for the Spirit: the *paraclete*.

This term comes from the Greek word *paraklētos*, which translates to "helper," "comforter," "advocate." This is the word Jesus uses in John's Gospel on the night before his death, when he promises his disciples that they will not be left alone:

> And I will ask the Father, and he will give you another Advocate, to be with you forever. This is the Spirit of truth, whom the world cannot receive because it neither sees him nor knows him. You know him because he abides with you, and he will be in you. (John 14:16–17)

When we think about the work of the Spirit, we might draw a picture that looks something like this:

This drawing—one person helping another to cross the street—helps us remember that the Spirit, this trinitarian person, is our guide: the very Advocate promised by Jesus in an upper room many centuries ago, the one who filled the disciples while they were together in another room after Jesus had ascended.

Of course, the Spirit wasn't "born" on that Pentecost day or awakened after eons of slumber. The Spirit has always been at work in the world. Think back to that final line in the section about the Spirit in the Nicene Creed: the Spirit "has spoken through the prophets." There are many places in the Scriptures we can point to where the Spirit is at work before his famous coming at Pentecost.

In the Old Testament, we see instances where the Spirit "comes upon" someone: "the spirit of God came upon Saul in power" (1 Sam 11:6); "the spirit of the LORD came upon him, and he judged Israel" (Judg 3:10).[4] In the New Testament, we can look at Luke's Gospel for an example of a Spirit-saturated, pre-Pentecost world. The Holy Spirit shows up a *lot* in Luke, empowering Jesus' ministry—even before he was born! When Mary is newly pregnant with Jesus, she visits her relative Elizabeth, who is pregnant with John the Baptist. Luke tells us that

4. Both of these examples listed in Welker, "The Holy Spirit," 237.

when Elizabeth heard Mary's greeting, the child leaped in her womb. And Elizabeth was filled with the Holy Spirit and exclaimed with a loud cry, "Blessed are you among women, and blessed is the fruit of your womb." (1:41–42)

The Spirit has been at work for a long time. As Beth Felker Jones writes, "The Spirit works in the Old Testament and the New, during the earthly life of Christ and after the ascension, in biblical times and today. The Spirit is not absent before Pentecost or after it."[5]

As Christians, though, we do believe that something world-changing happened on the day of Pentecost. When the Spirit filled the disciples that day, "a new knowledge of God and a renewal of spiritual insight and proclamation" came forth.[6] The theologian Michael Welker writes that "the event of Pentecost gives expression to God's intention towards all human beings. . . . Without eliminating the differences of languages and traditions, everybody is able to understand 'the mighty works of God.'"[7] The Spirit had not been missing from the scene before Pentecost, but the events of that day marked a shift in humanity's relationship with the Spirit—with God himself.

The Spirit-empowered life

In light of that seismic Pentecost shift, how do our lives look? What does a life in the Spirit look like?

In the chapter on anthropology, we learned about how we human beings are image bearers, "little images" of God. As embodied image bearers, we must live a Spirit-empowered life. A Spirit-empowered life is one marked by some very famous fruit.

Paul, in his letter to the Galatian church, wrote about what a life lived by the Spirit looks like:

The fruit of the Spirit is love, joy, peace, patience, kindness, generosity, faithfulness, gentleness, and self-control. . . . If we live by the Spirit, let us also be guided by the Spirit. Let us not become conceited, competing against one another, envying one another. (Gal 5:22–23a, 25–26)

5. Jones, *Practicing Christian Doctrine*, 189.
6. Welker, "The Holy Spirit," 238.
7. Welker, "The Holy Spirit," 238.

If you've grown up in the church, you've probably heard these verses a few times—maybe so many times that they've started to lose their meaning. Paul's description of a Spirit-filled life tells us that it will be evidenced by our behavior, by how we treat one another and ourselves. A life empowered by the Spirit is one that produces an abundance of good words and works and ways of being in the world. In other words, it's not exactly what we think of when we think of the word "spiritual"—if, by "spiritual," we mean "disembodied," "ethereal," etc. But it's what we *should* expect when the Spirit shows up.

The theologian Amos Yong writes about what to expect from a "Spiritual" experience, using the story of Mary's visit with Elizabeth in Luke's Gospel:

> First, the gift of the Spirit produces joy, but one that is embodied rather than disembodied. The arrival of the Spirit is thus never a merely "spiritual" occasion. Rather, Elizabeth receives the Spirit in the very depths of her being, touching even upon the child she is carrying in her womb. Hence the charismatic life is palpable, tangible, and kinesthetic, at least as Elizabeth experienced it.[8]

Yong helps remind us that a Spirit-filled life is not just an intellectual, disembodied experience. It's a fully embodied one, as we see in Elizabeth's example. She receives the Spirit, and something physical and concrete happens: John, her unborn baby, leaps in her womb. This is just more proof, as we saw in our Christology chapter, that the human body—that *all matter*—matters to God.

If we're living our lives by the Spirit, we should also expect the unexpected. The Holy Spirit is our promised helper, yes—but our God is also a God of justice and surprise.

Yolanda Pierce is the dean of Howard University School of Divinity. Her book called *In My Grandmother's House: Black Women, Faith, and the Stories We Inherit* describes the rich theological lessons she received from her church mothers, including lessons about the Holy Spirit as both Comforter and Disrupter.

> The Holy Ghost as Comforter was a gentleman, a sweet and gentle spirit. And yet the church mothers reminded me that the Holy Ghost was a Disrupter, too—a being who, through signs and wonders, unknown tongues and bodily praise, could disrupt a worship service or stop a sermon or bring forth an unsolicited

8. Yong, "The Gifts of the Holy Spirit," 59.

testimony. These Black church mothers had a highly developed pneumatology—although that fancy academic term for the theology of the Holy Spirit would never have crossed their lips. They were true trinitarians. That is, the Holy Ghost was not the neglected stepchild of the Trinity, as it is throughout many ecclesial spaces; it was an active and engaged power. The gifts of the Spirit—including healing, miracles, prophecy, tongues, and the interpretation of tongues—were spiritual works that I regularly witnessed in my childhood. For those living on the underside of history, for the disenfranchised and dispossessed, for the "least of these," the Holy Ghost can supernaturally disrupt time and space and miraculously make a way out of no way.[9]

Pierce's words remind us that while the Spirit is our comforter, we shouldn't get too cozy or comfortable—because, as Jesus himself said, the Spirit blows wherever he chooses, and we, not knowing where he's coming from or going, just have to be swept along.

We'll finish up this whirlwind pneumatology tour, but not before one more quick word from Barbara Brown Taylor. In a sermon she preached on Pentecost, she talks about the quality scholarship that's out there about the Holy Spirit (we might have even looked at some of it in this chapter!). But look at what else she says:

> There is some very fine teaching available on the Holy Spirit, and I hope none of you is satisfied with it. I hope none of you rests until you have felt the Holy Spirit blow through your own life, rearranging things, opening things up and maybe even setting your own head on fire.[10]

As we turn to learn more about the doctrine of salvation, may we keep Taylor's hopes in mind. May we not be satisfied with learning the right terms, the right names to quote, the right words of the Creed. Instead, may all of this make us ever more in awe of the God—Father, Son, and Holy Spirit—we love to learn more about.

---

9. Pierce, *In My Grandmother's House*, 69.
10. Taylor, *Home by Another Way*, 145.

8

Salvation: your best life later—and now!

Soteriology

When I (Tyler) was a kid, I sometimes had people explain only one part, but not the whole story, of salvation. Usually, people told me that salvation was like crossing a bridge into the afterlife, or sometimes it was like being in a lifeboat. Regardless of the metaphor, salvation was usually spoken of as *going to some other place*.

And those metaphors are fine, don't get me wrong. But *soteriology*—the doctrine of salvation—is about far more than just escaping this life and being rescued into the next. It's about God's power breaking right into our present circumstances, too.

Salvation is a gift from God. When we think of the word "salvation," it should make us grateful. But it's one of those church words that gets used so often that it loses its meaning. So in this chapter, we'll write (and sketch!) about what salvation is, how we are saved, and what the doctrine of salvation means for us in this life and in the next.

What is salvation?

The simplest definition of salvation is this: salvation is how God attaches his life to ours. And as we'll see throughout this chapter, when God attaches his life to ours, it changes our life. When God saves us, it frees us to be like God in this life and to be with God in the next.

But first, a sketch of what it means to be saved.

In this picture, we can see a person in the water behind a ski boat. They haven't started waterskiing yet—they're just plunked down in the water.

God is the boat driver. We are the skier in the water. Without God's salvation, we are stuck in that cold water. In order to experience the joy of salvation, we need God's help. And help is precisely what God does.

Like a waterskier receiving a handle that attaches them to a strong and powerful boat that pulls them up out of the water, God attaches himself to us, and with great power, saves us.

There are a few observations we want to make here. First, when the person is in the water, they are curled up in a ball.

Before God's salvation comes, the person is all alone, curved in on themselves, in a state of sin. (Remember the hamartiology chapter?) In a state of sin, we cannot grow into the creatures of love God wants us to be.

Second, God takes the initiative in our salvation. Salvation is a divine act, not a human act.

I (Tyler) used to work at a summer camp in Wisconsin, and one of my jobs was teaching kids how to waterski. I always said, "Let the boat do the work. Don't try to pull yourself up." The boat is strong and powerful, and if skiers try too hard to pull themselves up, they'll lose their balance and fall over. To be saved, we must let God do the heavy lifting, trusting that God loves us enough to save us. We don't have to save ourselves!

Third, waterskiing—and salvation—is supposed to be fun. When the boat roars and pulls you up, you are free to glide along the water. You can turn and feel the water with your hands, feel the wind against your face, and wave to others as you pass by.

Likewise, salvation is joyful. To be saved doesn't mean we sing worship songs all day and act like nice kids in Sunday School. To be saved means *we get our life back, the one God intended us for.* With God, our work can be productive and not simply fruitless toil, and our joy can be pure and simple, not just a distraction from reality. God's saving power puts us back in the position of being God's images in the garden, capable of giving and receiving love like we were meant to.

Once God attaches to us, we are free to be like God—to take great joy in the world. God frees us from a selfish, sinful, monotonous life so that we can learn to be like God in this life.

Gustavo Gutiérrez writes,

> To be saved is to reach the fullness of love; it is to enter into the circle of charity which unites the three Persons of the Trinity; it is to love as God loves. The way to this fullness of love can be no other than love itself, the way of participation in this charity, the way of accepting, explicitly or implicitly, to say with the Spirit: "Abba, Father" (Gal. 4:6). Acceptance is the foundation of all communion among human persons. To sin is to refuse to love, to reject communion and fellowship, to reject even now the very meaning of human existence.[1]

God saves us from a life of selfishness so that we are free to grow in love. Salvation is the cure for our state of sin. As we learned in the last chapter, sin isn't just a particular wrong behavior—*it is a state of being*. And salvation is how God corrects that selfish state of being. With love and tenderness, God pulls us out of ourselves and opens us up to one another so that we *can* love, accept communion and fellowship, and accept the very meaning of human existence.

How?

But how does God do this? How does God attach himself to us and free us to love? The answer is that God makes our condition his own. When we were trapped in a state of sin, God didn't simply yell at us and tell us to try harder. God helped us.

Back to our waterskiing analogy: it's worth mentioning that learning how to waterski is *hard*. I (Tyler) grew up in a family of skiers, and it took me years to learn how to do it. But I didn't learn by receiving lectures from my parents. I didn't sit in a classroom and take notes on how to ski. I learned how to ski because my mom got in the water with me.

My mom used to get in the water with me and make sure I was holding the rope correctly. She made sure my knees were tucked just right, that my arms were straight, and that my balance was correct. Once everything was set, she'd tell my dad (the boat driver) to "hit it!"—and I was off. My mom would then cheer like crazy, watching me zoom down the river.

1. Gutiérrez, *Theology of Liberation*, 113.

That's what it's like when God saves us. God didn't just give us instructions on how to be saved. Jesus, in the incarnation, makes our condition his own.

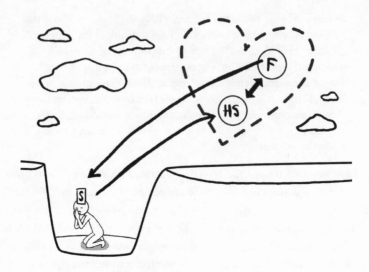

The Second Person of the Trinity chose to become like us. "The Word became flesh and lived among us," says the Gospel of John (1:14). God chose to attach himself to us when Jesus became a human being. As we saw back in the Christology chapter, in order to save us, Jesus became human, subjecting himself to all the things you and I go through. He became sleepy, he probably became hangry, and when he was a teenager in Nazareth learning the family business of carpentry, he probably got zits, too. He understands all the glory and misery of what it means to be a human being, including death. Jesus did all of this so he could understand our condition.

But it's important that we don't skip through Jesus' death on a Roman cross too quickly. His death is really, really important, because it is his ultimate identification with us as humans. More than that, it is also his supreme act of obedience to the other persons of the Trinity, the Father and the Spirit. The writers of the four Gospels (Matthew, Mark, Luke, and John) deem Jesus' death to be so essential to our salvation that each of them dedicates a large portion of their accounts of Jesus' life to his suffering and death. And why? Because it's a massive part of the explanation as to "how" we are saved.

Jesus himself was aware of the importance of his death. It doesn't seem to catch him by surprise. Throughout much of the Gospel of John, Jesus himself says that his "hour" has not yet come. As the story of Jesus' three-year earthly ministry unfolds in John's telling of Jesus' story, it becomes clear that his "hour" is his death. And then, his "hour"—his death on a cross—arrives.

Before his crucifixion, Jesus is in a garden called Gethsemane in Jerusalem. It's late at night. He asks his disciples to pray for him, because he knows the suffering he must endure. The disciples fail, falling asleep instead of praying for Jesus. The writers of the Gospels describe Jesus as being anxious, anguished even, as he pleads with the Father and says, "My Father, if this cannot pass unless I drink it, your will be done" (Matt 26:42). If there's any other way to save wayward humanity—and all of creation, for that matter—Jesus wants to hear about it. He knows that his death will be brutal, painful, and unjust.

After wrestling with this final aspect of his earthly mission, Jesus is obedient. When soldiers come to arrest him, he goes peacefully. He is silent before his accusers. Even though he is brutally tortured and killed by the Romans, he, "for the sake of the joy that was set before him endured the cross, disregarding its shame" (Heb 12:2). Before he breathes his last, he offers us another glimpse of the love that emanates from the heart of the Triune God. He says, "Father, forgive them, for they do not know what they are doing" (Luke 23:34). He dies.

And we should pause here. Jesus didn't only die for us, but he remained dead for us for three days. The Son of God, choosing to fully experience our humanity in order to save us, descends to the dead. His body is placed in a tomb, with a stone rolled in front of it.

The death of Jesus begs the question—why? Isn't there any other way that God could achieve our salvation? This goes back to what we mentioned in the chapter on Christology—that, as the early church theologians remind us often, "only what has been endured is healed and saved." In God's good pleasure, he chose to descend all the way to the depths of death in order to save us, to fully experience our humanity and redeem it.

But Jesus isn't just sympathetic to the human condition. He's powerful, too. After Jesus submitted himself to the ultimate form of human weakness, death, he was raised back to life through the other persons of the Trinity— the Father and the Spirit. Jesus then ascended to the Father, and right now he is speaking words of love on our behalf.

Again, think back to the Christology chapter: when Jesus chose to become like us in the incarnation, it wasn't a one-time choice, a rescue operation. The incarnation was a *permanent* choice, because right now, Jesus still has his human body. He still looks like his mom. This means that *our flesh and our life is forever attached to God.* Salvation is permanent. God's fundamental demeanor toward us is that of kindness—he doesn't change his mind about us. When God attaches himself to us, he stays loyal to us forever.

Salvation isn't something we can earn or receive. All we can do is say, "Thank you." As the beloved children of God, it makes God happy to free us from a sinful state. God wants to set us free to be like him in this life and to be with him in the next.

The wonderful thing about salvation, too, is that it isn't just something that affects our life after we die. Salvation begins right here, the moment we are free to love like God, and it becomes evident in the loving ways we learn to relate to God, others, and the world.

What does salvation mean for us?

When God saves us, it has practical implications for our life here on earth. Before we are saved, we are trapped in a state of sin: selfish, curved in on ourselves, not reaching the fullness of love. Salvation changes us, freeing us to become more like God.

Theologian Colin Gunton writes that "freedom in the [S]pirit is the God-given freedom to be like God in learning to love even the unlovely."[2] When we are saved and become free to be like God, we must be clear: God doesn't necessarily love the things that we find lovely.

Many people love things that are easy to love. Ice cream, for example, is really easy to love. Who doesn't like ice cream? (Well, maybe folks who are lactose intolerant.) Our friends are easy to love. Our hobbies are easy to love. I could go on, but you get the point.

God, however, loves what we find to be unlovable. God loves God's enemies. Paul writes in Romans 5:8, "But God proves his love for us in that while we still were sinners Christ died for us." So when God saves us, we are free to follow God's example of loving even our enemies. In Matthew 5, Jesus says,

2. Gunton, *The Christian Faith*, 156.

You have heard that it was said, "You shall love your neighbor and hate your enemy." But I say to you: Love your enemies and pray for those who persecute you, so that you may be children of your Father in heaven, for he makes his sun rise on the evil and on the good and sends rain on the righteous and on the unrighteous. For if you love those who love you, what reward do you have? Do not even the tax collectors do the same? And if you greet only your brothers and sisters, what more are you doing than others? Do not even the gentiles do the same? Be perfect, therefore, as your heavenly Father is perfect (vv. 43–48).

When we are saved, we are changed. You cannot have an encounter with the living God and be the same.

So far, we've mostly written about how salvation is a *private* phenomenon, meaning that salvation affects how we interact with others on an individual level, or how we interact with God. But that's only part of the story. Salvation is also a *public* phenomenon, meaning that it also leaves us changed in regards to how we interact with the systems of the world, things like governments and societies and businesses.

Author and teacher Megan K. Westra writes,

When salvation is a strictly personal, spiritual business between an individual and God, it lacks muscle sufficient for standing up against the systemic suffering of humanity.

It is far easier to tell a vibrant and compelling story about being converted and experiencing Jesus living "in your heart" than it is to pick up your cross and follow Christ in working against systemic suffering. If Jesus lives in your heart, he is close enough to comfort and guide, but small enough that he doesn't really mess anything up. If Jesus is in my heart, he can be in there for a long time convicting and purifying me but never touching the way I treat my neighbor, the way I manage my finances, or the way I vote. If my relationship with Jesus is merely a label for a deeply felt, but purely private, religious faith, then I can spend my whole life investing in building a kingdom without ever considering if I'm supporting the kingdom of God or an empire of this world. . . . If we enter into a personal relationship with God but stop there, we experience the theological equivalent of visiting someone's home but refusing to go any further than standing in the doorway and insisting that the way we enter is in fact the whole thing.[3]

---

3. Westra, *Born Again and Again*, 40–41.

Like Westra writes, salvation has a profound impact on our public lives, too. And since salvation changes us to be like God in *this* life, it may lead us to make some choices that make others scratch their heads.

Many of us spend a lot of our lives working very hard to avoid suffering. We get high-paying jobs so we can live in nice neighborhoods, and we send our kids to good schools so they can enjoy success and material prosperity, too. But living only for our comfort isn't like God.

Liberation

Author and civil rights activist Bryan Stevenson encourages us to get proximate to suffering in the world.[4] After all, Jesus left the comforts of heaven when he put on our flesh in order to save us, and he didn't spend his life on earth cozying up to the rich and powerful. We should get close to the poor, the lonely, and the marginalized—because that is what God does. Remember: a bad life is not one in which we suffer or grieve. A bad life is one in which we do not love. Indifference to the suffering of others is precisely the same as not loving as we should.

For that reason, you will often hear theologians write about *liberation* being at the core of the Christian tradition. When Jesus begins his ministry in his hometown of Nazareth, he quotes the prophet Isaiah, saying, "The Spirit of the Lord is upon me, because he has anointed me to bring good news to the poor. He has sent me to proclaim release to the captives and recovery of sight to the blind, to set free those who are oppressed, to proclaim the year of the Lord's favor" (Luke 4:18–21).

Jesus didn't only come to attach himself to our life, as wonderful as that is. Jesus came to fundamentally disrupt the structures that bind and oppress humanity. So for those of us who follow in the example and power of Jesus, part of being saved means working to liberate one another from the structures that harm us. In fact, theologian James Cone wrote that "any theology that is indifferent to the theme of liberation is not Christian theology."[5]

Certain theologians have been incredibly helpful in aiding our understanding of how our salvation is intimately tied to the liberation of all of humanity. James Cone has written extensively about the oppression that Black folks face in the United States. Gustavo Gutiérrez has written

4. Stevenson, *Just Mercy*, 14.
5. Cone, *Black Theology*, xxix.

about the oppression of Latin Americans (and many other folks in the Global South) at the hands of the industrialized North. These theologians help us to realize that if God attaches himself to us just to take us to heaven, but has nothing to do with the current plight of humanity, then God isn't that helpful.

But God *does* care about the liberation of the oppressed, and we should, too. To be saved, to be attached to Christ, forces us to rethink our relationship to the powers that oppress others. So when we notice economic relationships that generate wealth while taking advantage of others, or particular practices that favor one racial group while harming another, we must oppose them.

A friend once told me (Tyler) that "love isn't love if it isn't angered by injustice." It is impossible to be saved—to love like God in this life—if we do not seek the liberation of ourselves and others. Salvation is not a private matter.

Salvation in the next life

Salvation, as we defined it earlier, is when God attaches his life to ours and frees us to be like God in this life and with God in the next. Christian theology says that because Jesus passed over from death into life, then we will too, since we are attached to him. Jesus' resurrection is a template for our life after death. In 1 Corinthians 15:20–22, Paul writes, "But in fact Christ has been raised from the dead, the first fruits of those who have died. For since death came through a human, the resurrection of the dead has also come through a human, for as all die in Adam, so all will be made alive in Christ."

Paul explains that in Adam (the first human being), we have all been stained by sin, caved inward on ourselves. Sin stained us, but Jesus restored us and brought us back into friendship with God. And because our bodies are attached to Jesus' body, we too will be raised by the power of the Father and the Spirit to enjoy life even after death, in perfect friendship with God and others.

When God attaches himself to us and saves us, it changes us. We are free to love like God, to love even the things others say are unlovable.

Conclusion

My (Tyler's) grandparents modeled to me what it looked like to be saved, to be free to love like God in this life and to be with him in the next. They were ordinary people, but they had extraordinary love. When my grandpa was younger, he had the chance to go to college and become an accountant. He almost certainly would have earned far more money. But this would have pulled him away from his responsibilities to his aunts and uncles on their family farm. So he stayed. He worked at the *Daily News*, a newspaper in Iron Mountain, Michigan, for his whole career. He was a present dad and a loving husband. He had coffee with his same group of friends for most of his life. He was hospitable and gentle, mentoring teenagers in his church for nearly forty years. He served others. He cleaned up after others. He may not have been wealthy or successful in the world's eyes, but he was happy, because he was a man of remarkable love. He lived in friendship with others. He knew what it meant to be saved.

My grandma did, too. When my grandpa died, I'll never forget what it was like to be in that hospital room. When the doctor gave the official word that my grandpa had passed away, my grandma walked up to my grandpa's body, closed his eyelids, kissed his forehead, and said, "I love you, Ray, and I will miss you. But I will see you again." And then she sat down in her seat and she looked at me and my parents and said, "I guess the Bible is right. 'Where, O death, is thy sting? Where, O death, is thy victory?'"

I'm grateful that I read about the doctrine of salvation in a lot of books. But I'm even more grateful that my grandparents showed it to me. Their example shaped me into the person I am today.

Speaking of which, we'll now turn our attention to the church, the family of God that shapes and forms us so we can continue the work Christ began.

9

Let's talk about church

Ecclesiology

C hristianity is not a solo sport—it's a team effort.

In our culture, we often think of ourselves as individual persons. And on one level, that's correct. We are all unique. But we're also more than *just* individuals. We are all embedded in a web of relationships with our families, friends, environment, community, and country. It's impossible to understand who we are if we are unaware of the communities and environments that have made us who we are.

Theologically speaking, the group that shapes and forms us is the church. The word "church" is the English word usually used to translate the Greek word *ekklesia*, which means "gathering" or "assembly." The first Christians gathered together in homes as small groups in various cities throughout the Roman Empire. They met to praise God together, to ask God to assist them in their needs, to read Scripture and have it explained so they could orient their lives to the ways of Jesus, and to enjoy a common meal together.

These first Christians used a metaphor that helped them understand their purpose in gathering together as a group of Christians. They insisted that Jesus Christ was their "head" and that they were his "body."

Understanding this metaphor is essential in learning about the theological idea of the church, or *ecclesiology*. In learning about the church, we'll understand that the church's mission is to continue the work Christ began in his earthly ministry, and that in doing so, we can invite others to experience a unique way of being human.

The body of Christ

The apostle Paul writes in many places about the church as the body of Christ. First Corinthians 12:27 reads, "Now you are the body of Christ and individually members of it." Ephesians 1:22–23 reads, "And he has put all things under his feet and has made him the head over all things for the church, which is his body, the fullness of him who fills all in all." You get the picture—the apostle Paul and the first Christians used the metaphor of Jesus as the head and the church as the body *a lot*.

But what does that mean? What insights does this metaphor provide about the nature and purpose of the church?

In short, it means this: the church exists to continue the work that Jesus began in his earthly ministry. When we pay attention to the life of Jesus, we see that in his earthly life he delighted in the love of the Father and Spirit, and that he announced the coming of the kingdom. These tasks, then, become the task of the church.

Resting in the love of the Spirit and the Father

As the church continues the work of Christ, they must follow Jesus' example of delighting in the love of the Father and the Spirit. It's interesting to note that the four Gospels don't read like action novels. Jesus isn't a superhero who goes from task to task, miracle to miracle. Jesus is slow, contemplative.

There are so many occasions in the Gospels when Jesus goes away to pray, to experience solitude with his Father (Mark 6:30–32; Luke 5:16; 6:12; 22:39–44). In order to prepare for his ministry, to refresh himself after long periods of work, and to steady himself before his self-sacrifice on the cross, Jesus prayed. The Dutch priest Henri Nouwen writes,

> Who am I? I am the beloved. That's the voice Jesus heard when he came out of the Jordan River: "You are my beloved; on you my favor rests." And Jesus says to you and to me that we are loved as he is loved. That same voice is there for you. When you are not claiming that voice, you cannot walk freely in this world.
>
> Jesus listened to that voice all the time, and he was able to walk right through life. People were applauding him, laughing at him; praising him and rejecting him; calling "Hosanna!" and calling "Crucify!" But in the midst of that, Jesus knew one thing—I am the beloved; I am God's favorite one. He clung to that voice.
>
> There are many other voices speaking—loudly: "Prove that you are the beloved." "Prove you're worth something." "Prove you have any contribution to make." "Do something relevant." "Be sure you make a name for yourself." "At least have some power—then people will love you; then people will say you're wonderful, you're great."
>
> These voices are so strong in this world. These were the voices Jesus heard right after he heard "You are my beloved." Another voice said, "Prove you are the beloved. Do something. Change these stones into bread. Be sure you're famous. Jump from the temple, and you will be known. Grab some power so you have real influence. Don't you want some influence? Isn't that why you came?"[1]

Jesus refuses this temptation to frenetic activity. Jesus is not a workaholic. He rests. He prays. He listens to the voice of love coming from the Father and the Spirit. And we should, too.

It is a massive mistake to think that continuing Jesus' work here in the world entails frenetic activity. It doesn't. To be like God in the world we

---

1. Nouwen, "From Solitude," para. 13–17.

must first be with God—we must, like Jesus, find solitude and learn to hear his voice that calls us his beloved children.

The mother who bears and sustains us

But like I (Tyler) wrote at the beginning of this chapter, human beings are not as individualist as we sometimes think. We are communal creatures, people who *need* others. The task of hearing the voice that calls us God's beloved sometimes takes place in the context of solitude, but it often happens in the church.

Many theologians, including the German reformer Martin Luther, wrote that the church is "the mother who bears and sustains all believers." Before you think that's weird to imagine the church "bearing" us like a mother bears children, it's worth pointing out that throughout church history, most theologians have found it fitting to refer to the church as our "mother," usually utilizing female pronouns to speak of the church.

Some of you might be thinking, "Isn't the church the *body* of Christ? Now you're calling it 'mother.' How many metaphors are you going to use?" Well, to answer your question—just two. But the church is mysterious, so—like many other things in theology—multiple metaphors are needed to even begin to wrap our minds around it.

Christians call the church their "mother" because both the church and our earthly mothers give us life, nurture us, and teach us how to be in the world. As a matter of fact, an early church theologian named Cyprian said that "no one can have God as Father who does not have the Church as Mother."[2]

First, just like how our mothers give us birth, the church has a particular sacrament—baptism—that is our initiation into the life of the church. (The word *sacrament* means a physical sign of God's kindness. Depending on the church you worship in, you probably celebrate anywhere from two to seven sacraments, such as baptism and the Lord's Supper—those are the two we celebrate at our church. Part of what makes sacraments special is the fact that they take place in church, hence why we write about them in this chapter. But for now—more on baptism in particular.)

In baptism, people are welcomed into the life of the church. The pastor or priest either submerges the person in a pool of water or sprinkles water on the person's head. A lot of Christians have said a lot of things

2. Warren, "The Church," para. 3.

about the meaning of baptism, but what happens can be distilled down to two things.

First, the baptized person is marked with God's unconditional love. At our church, whenever someone is baptized, our priest says these words: "You are sealed by the Holy Spirit in baptism and marked as Christ's own forever." These words put a tear in my eye every time I hear them. Whether the baptized person is an adult or an infant doesn't increase or decrease the beauty of it. When it is a baby, it's a lovely sign that before this child can do anything good or bad, before they can follow Jesus or reject him, they are loved by God. God wants them. And when the baptized person is an adult, it's a marvel that nothing that this person has done or has had done to them can make them unlovable to God. Their past mistakes or pain cannot impede God's loyalty to them. As baptized persons, we are given new life in God—we are birthed into the life of the church. Through baptism, our new life is in Christ. We have union with him—just like Jesus, we are plunged into the waters of baptism, and we arise from those waters with new life in him. Our identity is new—we are marked as the beloved children of God.

Second, in baptism, the baptized person declares their intention to be a follower of Jesus. At our church, if the baptized person is an adult, they will be asked to renounce "the devil and all the spiritual forces of wickedness that rebel against God," "the empty promises and deadly deceits of this world that corrupt and destroy the creatures of God," and "the sinful desires of the flesh that draw you from the love of God." Further, they are asked to "turn to Jesus Christ and confess him as your Lord and Savior," to "joyfully receive the Christian Faith, as revealed in the Holy Scriptures of the Old and New Testaments," and to "obediently keep God's holy will and commandments."[3] If the baptized person is a baby, then the entire congregation takes these vows for the baby, promising to support and nourish the child—to teach them that following in the ways of Jesus is the best thing they can do with their life.

But following in the ways of Jesus can sometimes be difficult. We require help. That's a major reason why the church has her second sacrament: Communion, or Eucharist. This is the meal that Jesus gave us that nourishes and strengthens us in our life together. Some Christians believe that the Lord's Supper is literally the body and blood of Jesus. For others, the Lord's Supper is a memorial—a beautiful symbol. Many others see the meaning of the Eucharist somewhere on the spectrum between these two

3. Anglican Church, *Book of Common Prayer*, 164–65.

options. Regardless of exactly what you think happens when Christians celebrate the Eucharist, it's fair to say that every Christian agrees that the Eucharist strengthens us in our life with God.

That's because when we take the Eucharist together, we drink the blood of Jesus. We eat the flesh of Jesus. We do this so that our sinful bodies may be made clean by his body. Our flesh is weak—we are prone to sin. But God delights in joining himself to us, and that's exactly what happens in the Eucharist.

To continue with the metaphor of the church as our mother, many theologians have likened the Eucharist to a mother breast-feeding her child. Just like young babies require the tenderness and nourishment of a mother, we need the tender care of the church to nourish us in our life together. Living a life of love and sacrifice for others can sometimes be difficult—we need help.

Gustavo Gutiérrez writes, "This is the Eucharist: a memorial and a thanksgiving. It is a memorial of Christ which presupposes an ever-renewed acceptance of the meaning of his life—a total giving to others."[4] The life of the church, in continuing the mission of Christ, is to give itself for the world in love. We are nourished on this journey by none other than Christ himself. For this reason, the Eucharist is not sad or solemn—it is a feast of thanksgiving (in Greek, *eucharistia*), a declaration of the people of God that we are not alone.

I (Tyler) am fond of the metaphor of the church as our mother because I recall some of the advice my mom once received from one of her dear friends. Her friend said, "Your kids need you just as much at each phase of their life, just in different ways."

She's right. When I was a baby, I needed my mom to feed me and change my diapers. As a child, I needed my mom to love me, show me affection, and discipline me. As a teenager, I needed my mom to comfort me and challenge me. And now as an adult, I need my mom's advice and listening ear. I have never outgrown my need for my mom—but I need her in different ways today than I did when I was two.

Likewise, we *always* need the church, but in different ways throughout our journey of following Jesus. We need the church to comfort us when we mourn, to redirect us when we fall short of our calling of love, to forgive us when we fail. We never outgrow our need for our mothers,

<hr>

4. Gutiérrez, *Theology of Liberation*, 148.

and we always need the church to train us in the ways of Jesus so that we can continue his mission.

Announcing the kingdom

But Jesus' purpose and the church's purpose (which, remember, are closely bound) don't end at simply reveling in the love of God. Jesus announces that the kingdom of God is at hand—that the powers of this world are living on borrowed time. Jesus heals the sick, casts out demons, feeds the poor, and befriends the lonely. He is not simply a contemplative. He is an activist, too.

Jesus announced the presence of his kingdom through his actions. Likewise, the church, through her actions, can do the same.

Gutiérrez writes, "The point [of the church] is not to survive, but to serve. . . . The Church must be the visible sign of the presence of the Lord within the aspiration for liberation and the struggle for a more human and just society."[5] Gutiérrez warns us of the danger of forgetting that mission of the church, to continue the work of Christ.

Ecclesiology can quickly turn toxic if it turns inward and becomes too preoccupied with itself. (Wait, doesn't that sound a little bit like sin?) The church must follow in the example of Jesus, who came to serve: "For the Son of Man came not to be served but to serve and to give his life a ransom for many" (Mark 10:45). Again, Gutiérrez notes that "although the church needs human resources to carry out her mission, she is not set up to seek earthly glory, but to proclaim humility and self-sacrifice, even by her own example."[6]

In every community, there are unjust policies that need to be overturned, lonely people who need friends, and hungry people who need meals. Jesus announced the kingdom of God had arrived when he acted out against evil. And the church must shout out that these things are wrong, too, but we must shout in a Christlike way: by serving those around us.

5. Gutiérrez, *Theology of Liberation*, 148.
6. Gutiérrez, *Theology of Liberation*, 172.

An alternative community

When the church does this—when she delights in the love of God and grows in his likeness, and when she announces the coming of the kingdom through her actions, it will form the church into an alternative community in the midst of society.

That's a very high and holy way of saying this: if the church is faithful to her mission of continuing Christ's work in the world, she will be *weird*. The church will be misunderstood. There are certain values of Christianity that are just odd to the rest of the world.

When I (Tyler) was six, the 9/11 terrorist attacks happened. Shortly thereafter, the United States declared war on the Taliban in Afghanistan and overthrew their government. Meanwhile, at my home church, we prepared care packages and gifts for the children whose lives were overturned by the war. While many in America were viewing people in Afghanistan as our enemies, my church chose to pray for them and provide them with gifts. Christ was not violent, but peaceable, and his church should be, too.

Forgiving our enemies isn't the only calling of the church that may be perceived as odd by others. The church is governed by hope, trusting that the God who made the world will bring it to a good end. We refuse to be cynical. The church believes that money can never make us happy, so we happily give it away. Christians believe that we own nothing—that all we have is a gift from God, so we happily part with our possessions if it could benefit others. And Christians believe that our sexuality is best experienced in a context of faithfulness to one person only.

All of these distinctives of the church serve as an odd sort of invitation. The church is not called to be attention-seeking (Jesus was a humble carpenter, after all). Instead, the church is called to be filled with "patient revolutionaries," to borrow a phrase from Lesslie Newbigin. We are to practice our faith with sincerity and patience, and if our example is compelling to others, then we welcome them with open arms. A people who are marked by hope and not fear, patience and not anxiety, forgiveness and not bitterness, is quite compelling, I think.

There's an interesting story recorded in the Gospel of Luke. In it, Jesus sends out his disciples to heal the sick and preach the good news—but he sends them out in pairs (Luke 10:1). Couldn't they have reached more towns if they all split up and went to more villages?

But Jesus wanted his disciples to *model* what it means to announce the kingdom of God. He wanted others to see how his disciples treated the poor, how they resolved conflict among themselves, and how they put others' needs before their own. Jesus wanted their example to be compelling, to be something worth emulating. Commenting on this, Lesslie Newbigin writes, "Jesus . . . did not write a book, but formed a community."[7]

Newbigin also notes, "The only effective hermeneutic of the gospel is the life of the congregation which believes it."[8] That's a fancy way of saying that concepts like forgiveness, kindness, and justice are just that—concepts—until the church *embodies* them in their life together.

I (Tyler) had a professor in seminary, David Fitch, who frequently told us that "it's not our job to change the world—Jesus already did!" Instead, the role of the church is simply to be a physical sign that offers a better way forward. We may be embraced by some and rejected by others, and either of those responses is fine. After all, the church only *continues* the work of Christ. We do not complete it.

Christ's work is for him and for him only to finish. And he will. That's the subject of our next chapter: the chapter about how we all will live happily ever after.

7. Newbigin, *Gospel*, 172.
8. Newbigin, *Gospel*, 232.

10

Happily ever after

Eschatology

E *schatology* is the study of the end.

There are a couple different meanings of "end," and we're talking about both of them when we talk about eschatology. Eschatology has to do with the chronological end of the current state of creation, the end of history and time as we know them. It also has to do with the *ends* of creation, as in God's ultimate purposes and aims.

Eschatology is the field of theology that deals with "last things." When we study eschatology, we encounter God's final and ultimate "no" to the temporary powers of death, violence, and destruction. We see God's final and ultimate "yes" in declaring victory over those powers. Eschatology means that God wins, that God says "No more!" to evil.

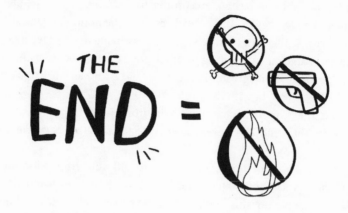

But in a world that seems so saturated with sin and death, that truth of God's ultimate victory can be hard to hold onto. As Christians, we find ourselves in an in-between space. We affirm Jesus' resurrection from the dead and his victory over death, and we anticipate our own bodily resurrection and the healing of creation. But we still look around and mourn the ways death rages around us.

This is a tension that Christian thinkers and scholars call *the "already" and the "not yet."* Jesus has *already* come, *already* triumphed—and how wonderful that is! But a quick glance at the headlines and our own lives will show that our bruised and aching world has *not yet* been fully redeemed and made whole.

So as people living in the midst of the "already" and the "not yet," we can look to eschatology for a glorious hope for the future—and some vital instructions on how to live in the present.

Future hope

By this point in the book, you might have been able to guess that the word "eschatology" comes from a Greek word—specifically *eskhatos*, or "last." In this first part of the chapter, we'll focus on the "last things" that Christians look toward as part of our faith.

When the texts that would eventually become the New Testament were being written, the whole concept of having amazing things to look forward to in the future was countercultural. The Roman Empire saw itself as the peak of civilization, having achieved a kind of prosperity that couldn't possibly be beaten. According to New Testament scholar Ross Wagner, the ideology of Rome "really resisted the notion of good things to come" because they saw themselves as already living in a "golden age": "[the Emperor] Augustus is bringing back the great days of the past, and no one can hope for anything greater in the future." The Roman story was one that said, "All is now right with the world."[1]

But the Christian story—both in Rome and today—dares to say something different. The Christian story declares that we have a *lot* to look forward to.

Take the book of Revelation, that weird and wonderful vision shown to John that closes out our Bibles. The disclosure of God's eschatological plan makes up the bulk of this book, as God's decisive "no" to evil and death is made plain over and over again.[2] We learn about the wedding feast of the Lamb and how all who are invited to it are blessed (19:7-9); we read that God "will dwell with [mortals]; they will be his peoples, and God himself will be with them and be their God; he will wipe every tear from their eyes. Death will be no more; mourning and crying and pain will be no more, for the first things have passed away" (21:3b-4). Isn't it hard to read those words without feeling a little pang in your chest? This is what we long for.

In Revelation, Jesus repeatedly reminds us that he is "coming soon"— because all of these hopes are bound up in what is known within the Christian tradition as the "second coming" of Christ.[3] The technical theological term for that second coming is a (you guessed it) Greek word, *parousia*, which translates to (you guessed it) "coming" or "presence." As the theologian and biblical scholar Richard Bauckham describes it, "The *parousia* will not be an event within history, but the event that brings history to an end." With the *parousia*, the ultimate reality of God's victory comes into clear focus: "the full and final achievement of God's rule over creation and . . . the unveiling of the full and final truth of all things."[4]

The word "unveiling" is a key one here because so much of eschatology concerns how, in the end, we will be able to see things rightly and clearly. We call this new sight *beatific vision*. This is the theological idea that one day we will encounter God directly, face-to-face.

1. Wagner, "Revelation."
2. Wagner, "Revelation."
3. Bauckham, "Eschatology," 318.
4. Bauckham, "Eschatology," 318.

You might be familiar with these lines from Paul's first letter to the Corinthian church:

> For now we see only a reflection, as in a mirror, but then we will see face to face. Now I know only in part; then I will know fully, even as I have been fully known. (1 Cor 13:12)

Paul's words here describe the concept of the beatific vision through the image of a mirror.

Right now, we see the world like we see our reflection in a mirror. We get to see some things, but not everything—we only ever see ourselves through our own eyes and according to the properties of that mirror.

The beatific vision, though, gets rid of the mirror. Instead of just seeing part of the picture, we see the whole thing. We come face to face with God, who is truth and love. We "know fully, even as [we] have been fully known."

Here's a word we need to keep in mind from those verses: *fully.*

At the end of all things, when we come to know as we have been known, we will see just how much is encompassed in the hope that we have. When God fully knows us, that knowledge includes our *particularities.* Remember the Christology chapter and the "scandal of particularity"—how Jesus is still in his own unique human body, which still shows his scars from the cross? Jesus isn't the only one whose particularities are preserved—far from it. In fact, Jesus' particular resurrected body means that our own particular bodies will be resurrected, as well.

Bauckham talks about this when he writes about how our eschatology must be holistic, including all of creation:

> Theologically a holistic eschatology is based especially on the bodily resurrection of Jesus. It was not that Jesus' spirit survived his death, but that his whole bodily person was raised by God out of death. The human body signifies interrelationship with other humans and continuity with the whole material world. Jesus' resurrection was in solidarity with the whole of this material, mortal, and transient reality and is therefore the promise that

everything of value in the present creation will be taken by God into his eternal life. . . . Nothing that is good in this world and its history will be lost.[5]

When God wipes away every tear and every pain, God will not do away with our bodies. We will not suddenly become a blank spirit in a homogenous mass of heavenly worshippers. Instead of a disembodied existence in the age to come, we will enjoy a thoroughly embodied resurrection.

The theologian and biblical scholar N. T. Wright describes our future existence like this: "It will be as much more real, more firmed up, more *bodily*, than our present body as our present body is more substantial, more touchable, than a disembodied spirit."[6] Far from being free of our bodies, we will instead find ourselves in bodies that are even *more* real than they currently are. What we currently experience is a shadow of what is to come.

But let's be absolutely clear: our resurrected bodies will bear the same markers of identity that they currently have. The book of Revelation describes this in glorious fashion:

> After this I looked, and there was a great multitude that no one could count, from every nation, from all tribes and peoples and languages, standing before the throne and before the Lamb, robed in white, with palm branches in their hands. They cried out in a loud voice, saying, "Salvation belongs to our God who is seated on the throne and to the Lamb!" (7:9–10)

John sees a big crowd before the throne, and notice what he tells us: that the people in it are "from every nation, from all tribes and peoples and languages." When it comes to the end, *our particularities will be preserved.*

The biblical scholar Esau McCaulley writes about this very passage in his book *Reading While Black*:

> This multitude . . . includes people from every nation, tribe, people, and language. Each in its own way highlights diversity. These distinct peoples, cultures, and languages are eschatological, everlasting. At the end, we do not find the elimination of difference. Instead the very diversity of cultures is a manifestation of God's glory.[7]

---

5. Bauckham, "Eschatology," 315, 319.
6. Wright, *Surprised by Hope*, 154.
7. McCaulley, *Reading While Black*, 115–16.

God's final "no" to evil and death is also a "yes" to the very differences and distinctions that make us who we are. Just as Jesus was not just Anybody from Anywhere, we will not simply be Someone from Somewhere in the age to come. We will be *ourselves*.

We've been talking about all the things we can know and hope for about the end based on the witness of the Scriptures and the truths revealed through the tenets of Christology. But there is so much—*so* much—we don't know. Lots of people have tried to read Revelation and other parts of the Bible as a kind of "field guide" to the end times—but that is decidedly *not* the purpose of those writings. When approaching biblical texts like Revelation, it's helpful to remember that we are not the community that was first being written to and addressed. The message of Revelation was meant to comfort those early Christians struggling with the apparent lack of divine justice in their world; through the visions of John, they could see God's ultimate victory.[8] Because we are *not* the original, intended recipients of this text, we must appreciate them and learn from them for what they are, and not as a play-by-play for the end of the world.

8. Wagner, "Revelation."

Let's turn to Richard Bauckham again, who reminds us that "probably more than any other aspect of theology . . . eschatology deals in the symbolic and the imaginative."[9] When Christians talk about the last things, we often will use language that talks about what *won't* be happening anymore (e.g., tears and pain and death) or that talks about how much *more* good will be happening in the age to come.[10] When we consider eschatology, we have to be imaginative. But this is not "mere speculation"; instead, "it is grounded in the promises of God and resourced by the images of scripture."[11] Even though there is much we cannot know for certain, we can rest in the hope of those promises and images.

But what about . . .

Before we turn to the ways this hope affects the way we live our lives in the here and now, we need to talk about the proverbial elephant in the room.

When we've talked about eschatology as the field that deals with "last things," what are the things that came to mind for you? We've probably touched on some big ones: heaven, resurrection, Jesus' second coming. But there are likely a couple other ones that you're wondering whether we'll get to: for instance, hell and judgment.

These are not the most comfortable topics, but they are still a part of eschatology—and they can still offer us future hope.

In this chapter, we've stressed how God will ultimately say "no" to all the powers of sin and death we see around us today. But what does that "no" entail? Judgment. Sin and death will not be let off the hook. "God's righteous judgment is part and parcel with God's promise of eschatological holiness and goodness," Beth Felker Jones reminds us, "and 'all of us must appear before the judgment seat of Christ' (2 Cor. 5:10)."[12] For those who have suffered, witnessed, and bemoaned the evils of this world, this is good news. Evil will not win, and evil will be judged. Remember Richard Bauckham's line a couple pages back, that "nothing that is good in this world and its history will be lost"? In the next sentence, he says:

9. Bauckham, "Eschatology," 316.
10. Bauckham, "Eschatology," 317.
11. Bauckham, "Eschatology," 317.
12. Jones, *Practicing Christian Doctrine*, 236.

But evil—the incomprehensible forces that ravage and destroy God's good creation—cannot survive God's perfecting of that creation. When the truth of all history is finally laid bare before the judgement of God, evil, as evil, must perish. This is not in contradiction to but is required by God's loving and salvific will for all his creatures. They must be delivered from evil.[13]

So evil, in the end, must—and will—perish. But what—and who—is included in that category of "condemned"?

This is where the question of hell comes in. Traditionally, Christians have thought of hell as the sentence given by God to those deemed guilty, "picturing the last judgement as a great assize where, following resurrection, all the living and the dead stand before Jesus the judge, who consigns the damned to hell and the redeemed to paradise."[14] But in this image, who constitutes the condemned? Who is damned and who is redeemed?

Plenty of theories attempt to answer those questions, some of them more comforting than others. A common theory has to do with free will and human choice, of "hell [as] justice in the face of recalcitrant refusal of God's loving offer of salvation."[15] In his famous fictional imagining of heaven and hell, *The Great Divorce*, C. S. Lewis has a key character describe hell in just that way:

> There are only two kinds of people in the end: those who say to God, "Thy will be done," and those to whom God says, in the end, "*Thy* will be done." All that are in Hell, choose it. Without that self-choice there could be no Hell. No soul that seriously and constantly desires joy will ever miss it. Those who seek find. To those who knock it is opened.[16]

But we would be amiss in including this quotation and claiming that this is exactly what Lewis believed about the afterlife. In fact, in his preface to *The Great Divorce*, Lewis wrote, "I beg readers to remember that this is a fantasy. . . . The last thing I wish is to arouse factual curiosity about the details of the after-world."[17] Lewis acknowledges the limits of our knowledge when it comes to death and judgment and hell, and thus joins a long line of thinkers and theologians who do not profess to know what exactly is

---

13. Bauckham, "Eschatology," 319.
14. Bauckham, "Eschatology," 319.
15. Jones, *Practicing Christian Doctrine*, 236.
16. Lewis, *The Great Divorce*, 75.
17. Lewis, *The Great Divorce*, x.

coming, but who have hope in a loving, merciful God. For instance, when it came to the question of who might be saved, Karl Barth "refus[ed] to limit the freedom of God," and Hans Urs von Balthasar "state[ed] that, while scripture and the church require us to believe that there is hell, they do not oblige us to claim that it must have inhabitants."[18]

There is much mystery here, and believe us, we wish we had the answers, too. "Living in eschatological expectation, we may be tempted to try to pin down our hope, to pretend to grasp all the specifics about God's ends in history," writes Jones.[19] But wrestling with the problems of evil, free will, and judgment, in Bauckham's words, "brings us very close to the limits of theological inquiry."[20] At those limits, may we find faith in a God who is both justice and love, "our Savior, who desires everyone to be saved and to come to the knowledge of the truth" (1 Tim 2:3–4).

Present action

Yet, as we talked about at the start of this chapter, eschatology not only gives us hope for a just and glorious future, it also tells us some important things about our lives *now*. When we know where the world is headed, that knowledge places ethical imperatives on us in the present. Our Christian hope is far from passive—it is active.

To talk about how and why that is, we'll learn one last technical theological term. Back in the creation chapter, we talked about the Latin phrase *creatio ex nihilo*, the concept of God creating out of nothing. When we talk about the new creation, the life everlasting, we use a different Latin phrase: *ex vetere*, or "from the old." In contrast with the beginning creation that was *ex nihilo*, the new creation will be *ex vetere*, as God will redeem and transfigure the current created order. As we've seen in this chapter, our bodies and our particularities will not be erased—and neither will this universe that God created, that God loves. Right now, creation is marred and hurting, and it's tempting to think that God will just burn it all down and start over. But the concept of creation *ex vetere* shows us that there is inherent value in the current created order, even in its brokenness.

The priest, physicist, and theologian John Polkinghorne wrote about this in his book *The Faith of a Physicist*:

18. Bauckham, "Eschatology," 319.

19. Jones, *Practicing Christian Doctrine*, 225.

20. Bauckham, "Eschatology," 320.

One immediate consequence of the new creation being *ex vetere* is that, quite contrary to the jibe about pie-in-the-sky, it invests the present created order with a most profound significance, for it is the raw material from which the new will come.[21]

Polkinghorne reminds us that God's new creation will not be "pie-in-the-sky," a radical discontinuity between creation as it currently stands and what is to come. Instead, God's new creation will transform and redeem the "raw material" of our current created order—which means we cannot deny its ultimate and everlasting value, even as we acknowledge its current brokenness. God will not wholly reject God's creation as God makes everything new.

So what does all this mean for us today?

Think back to the chapter on theological anthropology, on why we're here on this earth. The purpose of our lives is to be a small image of God's life. This is a wild and wonderful gift, which gives rise to wild and wonderful responsibility. If we're to image God, then we need to know what God is like and what God is up to. And when we study eschatology, we discover anew how much God loves God's creation—enough to resurrect and redeem our bodies and the world we live in. This has massive implications for us, because it means our bodies and our world are not simply going to

21. Polkinghorne, *Faith*, 168.

disappear when the new creation comes. Instead, at this moment, we are living in the building blocks of that new creation.

So how might we live our lives knowing that this world is "the raw material from which the new will come"? How might we take care of it, and take care of each other? What might our responsibilities be?

Conclusion

I (Emily) was talking with a friend who got engaged recently. We were discussing all things engagement—the proposal, wedding planning, dress shopping. After a while, my friend admitted that being engaged was more difficult than she thought it would be. There's a lot of waiting, wishing, wondering, wanting the wedding day and the new life together just to hurry up and arrive.

"Someone at my church described being engaged as like 'the already and the not yet,'" she said.

Doesn't that sound just about right?

As we live in this already-and-not-yet time, in a world that's hurting so much, we know we have the biggest of all marriage suppers to look forward to. Let's get ready for it.

Let's practice!

Conclusion

Y ou've done it! You've finished our whirlwind God-talk tour. Thanks for hanging in there.

But before we let you go, we need to give you a quick warning—and a reminder of why we do theology in the first place.

It might sound strange, but there's a real danger with learning more and more about God and all these doctrines and ideas and creeds. This kind of danger exists, to a certain extent, with learning more about any subject: the temptation to look down on people who haven't read what you've read, who haven't had the time or energy or interest. We think this temptation is particularly dangerous, though, when it comes to things of God—because this isn't just minds, but bodies and souls at stake.

So here's what we suggest: now that you've read this book (or any of the books we mention), it is not your job to email your pastor after every sermon with all the theological terms that were missing or points that could have been made. It is not your job to dismiss the questions or ideas your friends have about God. The point of learning about theology is not to go home and tell everyone how wrong they are. The point of learning about the Christian theological tradition is to be a more faithful follower of Jesus, the God-man who came in the form of a humble servant. This book is just a glimpse into the riches of that tradition, but we hope even that glimpse can help lead you to praise and wonder at our God.

But even with these caveats, we hope this book *does* show that there is a time and place for correction and criticism when it comes to theology. We hope that our discussions of creation, Christology, and more show there is much harm that can be wrought when certain doctrines are over- or underemphasized, or when too much airtime is given to white Western voices at the expense of our siblings in Christ who are so often skipped over. We hope that anyone reading this book will come away from it understanding that we need each other—the whole family of God—to know anything of what God looks and sounds and acts like. As Willie Jennings writes, "Our knowing is always as creatures, fragile creatures. We always understand in fragility. Which requires that we hold each other up in our striving to know, to understand, and to pay attention"—because in the end, the "central work" of any theological education is "to form us in the art of cultivating belonging."[1]

Remember, we all think theologically—with or without a seminary degree. As Yolanda Pierce reminds us, "Theological work cannot simply take place in academic spaces; it is not a dry set of questions to be posed by those who are 'qualified,' those who have a set of particular educational credentials. You do theology in community, and the best theology reflects the cares and concerns of that community."[2] We do theology in our everyday lives—that's the wonderful beauty of it. The theologian is no holier, no more valued by God, because they get paid to think Deep Thoughts. We all get to take part in this work, no matter our "day job," because everything in our lives is touched by God.

Janet Soskice, in her book *The Kindness of God*, writes about how "for many people the phrase 'the spiritual life' conjures up something still and luminous, turned to the future and far from our daily lives. . . . What we want is a monk who finds God while cooking a meal with one child clamouring for a drink, another who needs a bottom wiped, and a baby throwing up over his shoulder."[3] We believe that the search for God in

1. Jennings, *After Whiteness*, 59, 17.
2. Pierce, *In My Grandmother's House*, 83.
3. Soskice, *Kindness of God*, 12, 23.

the most mundane and tedious moments of our lives can be a fruitful search—which means that anyone in our lives can be a source of theological knowledge and truth.

So we'll end on this note: this book will only succeed if it makes you, the reader, a more loving person. As the pastor and writer Claude Atcho puts it,

> One way we have failed as God's people is that the presence of sound doctrine has made us overlook the absence of Christian love. . . . Jesus himself "was an extremist for love," to borrow Martin Luther King Jr.'s words. Christians are those who, from faith, strive in the power of the Spirit to become, in miniature, living icons of Jesus, extremists for love.[4]

May we never become so caught up in doctrine that we forget the reason all of it—the reason that anything in the universe—exists in the first place.

May this book lead you to more good books about theology—but, more importantly, may it lead you to love God and to love your neighbors.

4. Atcho, *Reading Black Books*, 52.

Recommended reading

General books on theology

The Oxford Handbook of Systematic Theology, edited by John Webster, Kathryn Tanner, and Iain Torrance.

Pocket Dictionary of Theological Terms, by Cherith Fee Nordling, David Guretzki, and Stanley J. Grenz.

Practicing Christian Doctrine: An Introduction to Thinking and Living Theologically, by Beth Felker Jones.

Dogmatics in Outline, by Karl Barth.

Chapter-specific books

TRINITY

Trinity Matters: In Faith, Work, and Love, by Steve Dancause.

The Christian Doctrine of God, One Being Three Persons, by Thomas F. Torrance.

On the Trinity, by Augustine.

CREATION

Church Dogmatics 3/1: The Doctrine of Creation, by Karl Barth.

Rescuing the Gospel from the Cowboys: A Native American Expression of the Jesus Way, by Richard Twiss.

REVELATION

Institutes of the Christian Religion, by John Calvin.

Revelations of Divine Love, by Julian of Norwich.

RECOMMENDED READING

CHRISTOLOGY

Christ the Key, by Kathryn Tanner.
Jesus Ascended: The Meaning of Christ's Continuing Incarnation, by Gerrit Dawson.

THEOLOGICAL ANTHROPOLOGY

After Whiteness: An Education in Belonging, by Willie James Jennings.
The Return of the Prodigal Son: A Story of Homecoming, by Henri Nouwen.

HAMARTIOLOGY

Lectures on Romans, Glosses and Schoilia, by Martin Luther.
Life Together, by Dietrich Bonhoeffer.

PNEUMATOLOGY

Paul, the Spirit, and the People of God, by Gordon Fee.
God, Sexuality, and the Self: An Essay "On the Trinity," by Sarah Coakley.

SOTERIOLOGY

A Theology of Liberation: History, Politics, and Salvation, by Gustavo Gutiérrez.
The Humanity of God, by Karl Barth.
Born Again and Again: Jesus' Call to Radical Transformation, by Megan K. Westra.
The Cross and the Lynching Tree, by James H. Cone.

ECCLESIOLOGY

The Gospel in a Pluralist Society, by Lesslie Newbigin.
A Community of Character: Toward a Constructive Christian Social Ethic, by Stanley Hauerwas.
Mission between the Times: Essays on the Kingdom, by René Padilla.

ESCHATOLOGY

Surprised by Hope, by N. T. Wright.

Discussion guide

We think that theology is at its best when discussed with others. To that end, we wrote a few questions you can use to discuss what you read about in *Napkin Theology*.

So who are we talking about? The triune God

Theologians have insisted on calling the Father, the Son, and the Holy Spirit the three "persons" of the Trinity. Why do you think this matters?

Since God loves God's self, we are free to become "co-lovers of God." We are not responsible for God's happiness, and we cannot add or subtract from it. Have you ever felt like you have been disappointing God? How does thinking of yourself as a "co-lover of God" affect the way you pray?

God is not a man and God is not a woman. God is, well, God—eternally existing as Father, Son, and Holy Spirit. Have you ever thought of God as the "big man upstairs"? Why do many people think of God like that?

A world made out of love: Creation

God doesn't *need* us, but God *wants* us. How does knowing that God doesn't need us—but that God instead delights in our friendship—change the way you relate to God?

Theologians believe that God created out of nothing. They call this concept *creatio ex nihilo*. Why do you think that is significant?

In this chapter, we read that "a weak theology of creation is bad news for creation. If we focus so much of our energy on ourselves as humans, on what God has done for us, and we don't pay much attention to the rest of the universe that God made, we end up staring at a tiny piece of the big picture that is God's love and care for the world." Have there been times when you have seen Christians prioritize humanity so much that they forget about the rest of God's creation?

Why—and how—does God tell us about God's self? Revelation

This chapter focuses on the four primary ways we receive God's revelation: Jesus, Scripture, tradition, and general revelation. Which of these four do you find to be the easiest way of receiving God's revelation? The hardest?

We don't possess truth; we pursue it alongside our brothers and sisters. What are some ways that you can learn more about God while not becoming arrogant?

In this chapter, we read, "Like a friend who writes letters, sends emails, makes personal phone calls, and visits in person, so too does God devise multiple ways of being known by us." Do you find that it is easy to pay attention to God when he tries to reveal himself? What helps you to pay attention to God?

The scandal of the Son: Christology

This chapter talks about "the scandal of particularity," the idea that Jesus was incarnate as a Jewish man in first-century Palestine under the Roman Empire. Does it bother you that Jesus has his own particular features and doesn't share every single particularity with us (e.g., our race, nationality, or gender)?

Jesus didn't just go on a "rescue mission" for us—putting on a human body, being perfect, dying, and being raised. He is our ascended older brother, who still is in a human body. Why does this matter so much?

Some of the first Christian theologians said that God the Father and God the Son were of the *same* substance, not just a similar substance. Why is this so important, and why did people fight so much about it?

Why are we here? Theological anthropology

The purpose of our life is to be a small image of God's life. Who are some people in your life who have done this well?

Since we are all made in the image of God and are called to bear God's image, it means that people should be treated with the utmost kindness and care. But often, we fail to do that. Why do you think we have such a hard time treating one another well?

Bearing God's image means that we are supposed to be like God, to be small images of God. We are called to imitate God, not others. But sometimes we compare ourselves to others. How can knowing our purpose in life help us be more content with ourselves and not compare ourselves to others quite as much?

Missing the mark: Hamartiology

In this chapter, sin is described as not simply a matter of breaking rules—it is a state of being. Do you agree or disagree with this?

When we are trapped in a state of sin, we harm others and ourselves. Why do you think it is important to understand sin not just as a philosophical idea, but as a real-world phenomenon that has consequences?

Sin is like "missing the mark." When you notice yourself in a state of sin, what are some ways you can make some changes but not beat yourself up too much?

Speaking of the Spirit: Pneumatology

Even though the Spirit can sometimes be a bit hard to describe, the church insists on calling the Spirit a "person." Why do you think it is important to speak of the Holy Spirit in relational, personal terms?

Yolanda Pierce wrote, "The gifts of the Spirit—including healing, miracles, prophecy, tongues, and the interpretation of tongues—were spiritual works that I regularly witnessed in my childhood." When have you seen the Holy Spirit do supernatural, wonderful things?

In this chapter, we read that "Paul's description of a Spirit-filled life tells us that it will be evidenced by our behavior, by how we treat one another and ourselves. A life empowered by the Spirit is one that produces an abundance of good words and works and ways of being in the world." The Holy Spirit is not purely "spiritual" but really helps us in our daily, embodied life. How have you seen the Spirit in your daily life?

Salvation: your best life later—and now! Soteriology

This chapter describes salvation like this: when we are saved, God attaches his life to ours, making us free to love like God in this life and to be with God in the next. Do you agree with this definition? Why?

When we are saved, we are free to love like God loves, and God loves even the things that we find unlovely. What things or people in life are hard for you to love, and how can God's saving power help you?

Tyler's friend once told him that "love isn't love if it isn't angered by injustice." How can God's saving power help us to fight for liberation here on earth?

Let's talk about church: Ecclesiology

The task of the church is to continue the work of Christ. Why is it important for the church to *continue*, and not necessarily to *complete*, his work?

In this chapter, we read that Jesus rested in the love of the Father, Son, and Holy Spirit, and that he announced the kingdom of God. What are some ways that your church today can continue that mission?

Tyler's professor used to say that "it's not our job to change the world—Jesus already did!" Do you agree with this statement or not?

Happily ever after: Eschatology

When you think about the end of the world, do you become excited, or afraid? Why?

This chapter tells us that "when we study eschatology, we discover anew how much God loves God's creation—enough to resurrect and redeem our bodies and the world we live in. This has massive implications for us, because it means our bodies and our world are not simply going to disappear when the new creation comes. Instead, at this moment, we are living in the building blocks of that new creation." How does it change your behavior when you know that God won't destroy this world and replace it with a new one?

The book of Revelation was first written to early Christians struggling in the midst of the Roman Empire. How does knowing we were not the book's first audience change the way you read it?

Glossary

Here you'll find the technical theological terms we've italicized and defined throughout the book, listed in alphabetical order.

Accommodation: A term that describes how, since we human beings are *very* different from God, God's revelation comes to us in ways that are appropriate and understandable to our human minds. Each method of revelation is an act of God's accommodation to us.

The "already" and the "not yet": A term for the in-between space we Christians find ourselves in, where we affirm Jesus' resurrection from the dead and his victory over death, and we anticipate our own bodily resurrection and the healing of creation. But we still look around and mourn the ways death rages around us.

Beatific vision: The theological idea that one day we will encounter God directly, face-to-face, and we will be able to see things rightly and clearly.

Chalcedonian formula: The Council of Chalcedon's concluding statement of faith, which describes Jesus' divine and human natures: "two natures without confusion, without change, without division, without separation—the difference of the two natures being by no means taken away because of the union."

Council of Chalcedon: An ecumenical council that met in 451 CE, which sought to affirm the right manner of speaking about Jesus' humanity and divinity. The council's concluding statement of faith has come to be known as the *Chalcedonian formula* (see above), which describes Jesus' divine and human natures.

Council of Nicaea: In 325 CE, this council met to sort through the ways we talk about the relationship between God the Father and God the Son. A teaching called Arianism was in the air, which scoffed at the idea that Jesus was *really* God. The Council of Nicaea quashed that thought. They declared that Jesus was *not* a created being, but that he and the Father were of one being: *homoousios* in Greek, with *homo* meaning "one" and *ousios* (ou-see-ahs) meaning "substance."

Creatio ex nihilo: A Latin phrase that translates to "created out of nothing," which theologians use to describe God's creation of the universe.

Ecclesiology: The theological idea of the church. This comes from the Greek word *ekklesia*, which is translated as "gathering" or "assembly."

Economic Trinity: The term for the Trinity in its relation to what is not God, in relation to what God has created.

Ecumenical councils: Gatherings of church leaders, coming together to figure out how to talk about God—because there were people whose God-talk was just a little off. (And by "just a little off," we mean way, way off.)

Eschatology: The field of theology that deals with "last things": Jesus' second coming, heaven, resurrection, etc. The word "eschatology" comes from the Greek word *eskhatos*, or "last."

Ex vetere: A Latin phrase that means "from the old." In contrast with the beginning creation that was *ex nihilo*, the new creation will be *ex vetere*, as God will redeem and transfigure the current created order.

Filioque: Latin term for "and the Son." Latin-speaking Western church leaders changed the Nicene Creed to read that the Spirit "proceeds from the Father *and the Son*." The Eastern church still does not recognize the *filioque* as part of the Creed.

Hamartiology: The study of sin. "Hamartiology" derives from the Greek word *hamartolos*, which is an archery term used to describe when someone shoots an arrow, but misses the mark.

Hypostatic union: The technical phrase used in theology circles for the concept of Jesus as both God *and* human, but with his God-ness and his humanness—while different and distinct—being intertwined and inseparable.

Immanent Trinity: The term referring to the inner life of the three persons of the Trinity, that dance of love that Father, Son, and Spirit spin and move in. When we say "immanent," we mean "internal," "innate," "inside." This is a pretty mysterious concept, because there's only so much we can know and say about what goes on inside the Godhead apart from what we can see in the world around us. (By "only so much" we mean "not a whole lot.")

Incarnation: The term we use to refer to the mystery spoken of by John: "the Word *became flesh* and lived among us" (John 1:14). The incarnation is God's "yes" to pockmarked, smelly, wonderfully made humanity.

Incurvatus in se: Latin for "curved inward on oneself." Seeking only themselves when in a state of sin, human beings fail to take great joy in others.

Munus triplex: The "threefold office" of Jesus as prophet, priest, and king. Jesus, as a sort of bridge between the Old and New Testaments, is the new Elijah, Aaron, and David.

Nicene Creed: The creed that emerged out of the Council at Nicaea, which spells out the relationship between Jesus and the Father in a strong rebuke of Arius and his teachings. Jesus is the Son of God and is *eternally begotten* of God, not a created being; Jesus and the Father are one, not two separate beings.

Paraclete: A name Jesus used for the Spirit. This term comes from the Greek word *paraklētos*, which translates to "helper," "comforter," "advocate."

Parousia: A Greek word that translates to "coming" and is the technical theological term for the second coming of Jesus.

Perichoresis: A Greek word that is difficult to precisely translate into English, but that means something like "delight," "mutual indwelling," or "endless joy." It describes the love that the Father, Son, and Holy Spirit have had for one another from eternity "past," even "before" the creation of the universe. This is a word we use to try and capture the idea that within the life of the Father, Son, and Holy Spirit, there is complete and unstoppable joy.

Pneumatology: The technical term for the study of the Holy Spirit. Why call it "pneumatology"? The Greek word *pneuma* means "spirit"—hence "pneumatology" as "Spirit study."

Processions: This term is what we use when we talk about the relationships between the persons of the Trinity. Unlike the Son, who is *begotten* from the Father, the Spirit is not begotten; rather, we say that the Spirit *proceeds* from the Father (and the Son, in Western theology).

Revelation: A catch-all word that encapsulates *how* and *why* God tells us about reality. God's revelation comes to us in four primary ways: Jesus Christ, the Bible, sacred tradition, and general revelation.

Sacrament: The word *sacrament* means a physical sign of God's kindness. Depending on the church you worship in, you probably celebrate anywhere from two to seven sacraments, such as baptism and the Lord's Supper.

Scandal of particularity: A phrase scholars use to talk about the mind-boggling reality of Jesus' first-century earthly existence.

Sin: A selfish state of being when a person is curved in on themselves, unable to love as they should. We human beings fall short of our calling to be images of God, time and time again. Theologically speaking, Christians call this failure to live up to our calling "sin."

Soteriology: The doctrine of salvation, which is about far more than just escaping this life and being rescued into the next. It's about God's power breaking right into our present circumstances. The simplest definition of salvation is this: salvation is how God attaches his life to ours.

Spirate: The technical term for the relationship between the Father and the Spirit; the Father spirates the Spirit, just as he begets the Son.

Supersessionism: The harmful belief that God has moved on from the Jewish people, casting them aside because of their rejection of Jesus. This idea says that the church is their replacement—as in, we can look at the Old Testament and simply plug in "the church" or "Christians" whenever we see references to Israel and the Jewish people.

Theology: "God talk"—whether it's God talking to us, us talking to God, or us talking about God and things related to God. The word "theology" comes from two ancient Greek words, *theos* and *logos*: *theos* means "God"; *logos* means "word."

Trinity: The doctrine of God as three in one. Really, whenever we say "God," we're using a shortcut word for "Father, Son, and Holy Spirit."

Bibliography

The Anglican Church in North America. *The Book of Common Prayer (2019)*. Huntington Beach, CA: Anglican Liturgy, 2019.

Atcho, Claude. *Reading Black Books: How African American Literature Can Make Our Faith More Whole and Just*. Grand Rapids: Brazos, 2022.

Balthasar, Hans Urs von. *Mysterium Paschale: The Mystery of Easter*. Translated by Aidan Nichols, OP. San Francisco: Ignatius, 2000.

Barth, Karl. *Church Dogmatics*. 1/1: *The Doctrine of the Word of God*. Translated by T. H. L. Parker et al. Peabody, MA: Hendrickson, 2010.

———. *Church Dogmatics*. 2/1: *The Doctrine of God*. Translated by T. H. L. Parker et al. Peabody, MA: Hendrickson, 2010.

———. "The Humanity of God." In *The Humanity of God*, 37–68. Translated by John Newton Thomas and Thomas Wieser. Louisville: Westminster John Knox, 1960.

Bauckham, Richard. "Eschatology." In *The Oxford Handbook of Systematic Theology*, edited by John Webster et al., 306–24. Oxford: Oxford University Press, 2009.

Begbie, Jeremy. "How Music Helps Explain the Trinity." Video, 5:52. June 15, 2016. https://seedbed.com/how-music-helps-explain-the-trinity/.

Bettenson, Henry, and Chris Maunder, eds. *Documents of the Christian Church*. Oxford: Oxford University Press, 2011.

Bonhoeffer, Dietrich. *Life Together: The Classic Exploration of Christian Community*. Translated by John W. Doberstein. New York: HarperOne, 2009.

Calvin, John. *Institutes of the Christian Religion*. Translated by Henry Beveridge. Peabody, MA: Hendrickson, 2008.

The Church of England. "The Apostles' Creed." https://www.churchofengland.org/our-faith/what-we-believe/apostles-creed.

Cone, James H. *A Black Theology of Liberation*. Maryknoll, NY: Orbis, 2020.

Cyril of Alexandria. *On the Unity of Christ*. Translated by John Anthony McGuckin. Popular Patristics Series. Yonkers, NY: St. Vladimir's Seminary Press, 2015.

Favale, Abigail Rine. *Into the Deep: An Unlikely Catholic Conversion*. Eugene, OR: Cascade, 2018.

Grenz, Stanley J., et al. *Pocket Dictionary of Theological Terms*. IVP Pocket Reference Series. Downers Grove, IL: IVP Academic, 2010.

Gunton, Colin E. *The Christian Faith: An Introduction to Christian Doctrine*. Malden, MA: Blackwell, 2001.

Gutiérrez, Gustavo. *A Theology of Liberation: History, Politics, and Salvation*. Translated by Sister Caridad Inda and John Eagleson. Maryknoll, NY: Orbis, 1988.

Hopkins, Gerard Manley. "God's Grandeur." https://www.poetryfoundation.org/poems/ 44395/gods-grandeur.

Jennings, Willie James. *After Whiteness: An Education in Belonging.* Theological Education between the Times. Grand Rapids: Eerdmans, 2020.

———. *The Christian Imagination: Theology and the Origins of Race.* New Haven, CT: Yale University Press, 2010.

Johnson, Keith L. "The Metaphysics of Marilynne Robinson." In *Balm in Gilead: A Theological Dialogue with Marilynne Robinson,* edited by Timothy Larsen and Keith L. Johnson, 66–84. Downers Grove, IL: IVP Academic, 2019.

Jones, Beth Felker. *Practicing Christian Doctrine: An Introduction to Thinking and Living Theologically.* Grand Rapids: Baker Academic, 2014.

Julian of Norwich. *Revelations of Divine Love.* Translated by Barry Windeatt. Oxford: Oxford University Press, 2015.

Lamott, Anne. *Traveling Mercies: Some Thoughts on Faith.* New York: Anchor, 2000.

Lewis, C. S. *The Great Divorce.* New York: HarperOne, 2015.

———. *The Weight of Glory.* New York: HarperOne, 2009.

Luther, Martin. *Lectures on Romans, Glosses and Schoilia.* Luther's Works 25. St. Louis: Concordia, 1972.

McCaulley, Esau. *Reading While Black: African American Biblical Interpretation as an Exercise in Hope.* Downers Grove, IL: IVP Academic, 2020.

Newbigin, Lesslie. *The Gospel in a Pluralist Society.* Grand Rapids: Eerdmans, 1989.

Nouwen, Henri. "From Solitude to Community to Ministry." *Leadership Journal* 16 (April 1995). https://www.christianitytoday.com/pastors/1995/spring/5l280.html.

Pierce, Yolanda. *In My Grandmother's House: Black Women, Faith, and the Stories We Inherit.* Minneapolis: Broadleaf, 2021.

Polkinghorne, John. *The Faith of a Physicist: Reflections of a Bottom-Up Thinker.* Princeton, NJ: Princeton University Press, 1994.

Robinson, Marilynne. *Gilead.* New York: Picador, 2005.

Soskice, Janet Martin. *The Kindness of God: Metaphor, Gender, and Religious Language.* Oxford: Oxford University Press, 2007.

———. "Why *Creatio ex nihilo* for Theology Today?" In *Creation Ex Nihilo: Origins, Development, Contemporary Challenges,* edited by Gary A. Anderson and Markus Bockmuehl, 37–54. Notre Dame, IN: University of Notre Dame Press, 2017.

Stevenson, Bryan. *Just Mercy: A Story of Justice and Redemption.* New York: One World, 2015.

Taylor, Barbara Brown. *Home by Another Way.* Lanham, MD: Cowley, 1997.

Tinker, George E. ("Tink"). "Creation, Justice, and Peace: Indians, Christianity, and Trinitarian Theologies." In *American Indian Liberation: A Theology of Sovereignty,* 36–56. Maryknoll, NY: Orbis, 2008.

Torrance, Thomas F. *The Christian Doctrine of God: One Being Three Persons.* London: Bloomsbury T. & T. Clark, 2016.

Wagner, J. Ross. "Revelation: The End of the Beginning." Lecture given as part of NT 754: New Testament Interpretation, Duke Divinity School, Durham, NC, April 2020.

Warren, Tish Harrison. "The Church Is Your Mom." *Christianity Today,* May 21, 2015. https://www.christianitytoday.com/ct/2015/may-web-only/church-is-your-mom.html.

Welker, Michael. "The Holy Spirit." In *The Oxford Handbook of Systematic Theology,* edited by John Webster et al., 236–48. Oxford: Oxford University Press, 2009.

Westra, Megan K. *Born Again and Again: Jesus' Call to Radical Transformation.* Harrisonburg, VA: Herald, 2020.

Wright, Christopher J. H. *Knowing Jesus through the Old Testament.* Downers Grove, IL: IVP Academic, 1995.

Wright, N. T. *Surprised by Hope: Rethinking Heaven, the Resurrection, and the Mission of the Church.* New York: HarperOne, 2018.

Yong, Amos. "The Gifts of the Holy Spirit: Christian Ministry and the Mission of God." In *Renewing Christian Theology: Systematics for a Global Christianity,* 57–80. Waco, TX: Baylor University Press, 2014.